S A R A H C O O K

PRACTICAL BENCHMARKING

A manager's guide
to creating a competitive advantage

KOGAN
PAGE

First published in 1995
Paperback edition published in 1997

Kogan Page Limited
120 Pentonville Road
London N1 9JN

© Sarah Cook, 1995

British Library Cataloguing in Publication Data
A CIP record for this book is available from the British Library
ISBN 0 7494 2227 0

Contents

List of Figures

Preface

Recent surveys across major countries indicate that over two thirds of leading companies are conducting benchmarking on a regular basis. Almost all of them are expecting to increase their investment in benchmarking over the next five years.

These results suggest that benchmarking will be a key management technique for the 1990s and beyond.

This book is written in response to the growing interest in the topic. The book aims to encourage recognition that benchmarking can be used as a stimulus and a tool to help transform business performance.

In addition to establishing the benefits of benchmarking, the book sets out the pitfalls and challenges of undertaking a benchmarking programme. It provides a step by step guide to undertaking the benchmarking process, as well as practical examples of benchmarking in action.

The final pages of the book provide information on benchmarking resources and a bibliography.

In order to assist the reader in being able to apply the principles set out in this book, each chapter ends with a summary and an action checklist so that readers can put their learning into practice.

I hope this book acts as a catalyst in the process of identifying, understanding and adapting outstanding practices to help improve business performance.

Sarah Cook
The Stairway Consultancy

1

What is Benchmarking?

Benchmarking is the process of identifying, understanding and adapting outstanding practices from within the same organisation or from other businesses to help improve performance.

This involves a process of comparing practices and procedures to those of the best to identify ways in which an organisation can make improvements. Thus new standards and goals can be set which, in turn, will help better satisfy the customer's requirements for quality, cost, product and service.

In this way, organisations can add value to their customers and distinguish themselves from their competitors.

Rank Xerox is an example of an organisation which has made extensive use of benchmarking.

Rank Xerox is part of Xerox Corp, a multinational company that found itself in deep trouble in the late 1970s. From the mid 1960s to the mid 1970s its profits rose 20 per cent a year, not least because it had a near-monopoly on photocopier technology. By 1980 it saw its market share halve, as aggressive competitors moved in and beat it on price, quality and other important measures.

Xerox's solution was to benchmark the way its photocopiers were built, the cost of each stage of production, the costs of selling, the quality of the servicing it offered, and many other aspects of its business against its competitors and against anyone else from whom it could learn. Whenever it found something that someone else did better, it insisted that the level of performance became the new base standard in its own operations.

Benchmarking has now become an everyday activity for every department in Xerox and Rank Xerox. The guiding principle is 'Anything anyone else can do better, we should aim to do at least equally well'. It is closely tied in to the company's quality management programme, because benchmarking is one of the most important ways of identifying where quality improvements are needed. Not only has Xerox world-wide improved its financial position and stabilised its market share, but it has increased customer satisfaction by 40 per cent in the past four years.[1]

WHY BENCHMARKING IS NEEDED

Benchmarking helps organisations focus on the external environment and improve process efficiency.

The number, extent and pace of changes in the external environment mean that no person or business can afford to be complacent. The increasing sophistication of marketplaces and rise in competition means that an organisation's competitive advantage is constantly being eroded as barriers to entry decrease.

In the course of twenty years the office environment has changed rapidly, for example. Computers, electronic mail and faxes have replaced typewriters and telexes. The skill sets required of the effective manager have also changed.

There has been a continuous shift towards flatter, non-hierarchical organisations. In the new working environment, greater emphasis has been placed on teamwork, involvement and continuous improvement. The output of this movement is a greater awareness of customer needs and a more commercial and competitive focus within organisations.

Benchmarking promotes a climate for change by allowing employees to gain an understanding of their performance – what they are achieving now and how they compare to others – in order that they become aware of what they could achieve.

THE BENEFITS OF BENCHMARKING

Benchmarking brings many advantages to an organisation:

- It sets performance goals.

- It helps accelerate and manage change.

- It improves processes.

- It allows individuals to see 'outside the box'.

- It generates an understanding of world-class performance.

THE ORIGINS OF BENCHMARKING

Benchmarking first emerged during the 1950s when benchmarks or standards were used to measure business performance in terms of cost/sales and investment ratios. This allowed businesses within particular industries to see how they compared with their peers and to identify their strengths and weaknesses.

However, the comparison of management ratios was based on past financial performance. The benchmarking techniques used at this time did not investigate the *practices* or *procedures* which led to the performance or how further improvements in performance could be achieved.

The growth of the computer industry throughout the 1960s and 1970s brought further developments in the use of benchmarking. The proliferation of suppliers and systems meant that a number of techniques were developed to assist the purchaser to measure and compare performance.

In the late 1970s, benchmarking of intangible as well as tangible management practices was driven by Rank Xerox to its great benefit, as we have seen in the example earlier.

The use of benchmarking grew rapidly throughout the US during the 1980s as many companies identified the need to improve the quality of their output and business performance. This development followed on from that of Total Quality Management (TQM). Benchmarking became a recognised tool in the development of a continuous improvement process. Indeed the prestigious American prize for quality, the Malcolm Baldridge award and its European equivalent, the EFQM, have incorporated benchmarking into its guidelines.

In this country benchmarking was a relatively unknown and unapplied technique until the late 1980s. UK companies with US connections began benchmarking during the early 1990s. So organisations such as Rank Xerox, Digital Equipment Company and Milliken Industrials (UK) used and continue to use the technique as an integral part of their corporate strategy.

The first benchmarking seminar was held by the British Quality Association in 1991. Increasing interest and use of benchmarking by companies in the UK has led to numerous conferences and seminars on the topic. In addition, companies such as Royal Mail and Rover Cars have shared their experience of the benefits of benchmarking via the creation of benchmarking clubs and circles. These meet on a regular basis to exchange information and provide help and guidance to companies planning to undertake the benchmarking process.

In the UK, the Department of Trade and Industry (DTI)

is also actively encouraging the use of benchmarking throughout industry (see Sources of Further Information).

OVERVIEW OF THE BENCHMARKING PROCESS

Benchmarking is an on-going process which requires a systematic approach. There are six discrete steps to effective benchmarking.

Figure 1.1 *Six steps in the benchmarking process*

This book outlines the phases of each step in the process and provides practical guidance on how to undertake each step.

TYPES OF BENCHMARKING

There are four types of benchmarking which can be undertaken by an organisation:

17

1. internal;

2. competitive;

3. non competitive; *and*

4. best practice/world class.

Internal

This is the easiest type of benchmarking to conduct since it involves measuring and comparing company data on similar practices from other parts of an organisation, one branch office with one another, for example. Internal benchmarking creates an environment of two-way communication and sharing within an organisation. It also overcomes any problems of confidentiality and trust.

Centre Parcs, the leisure company, benchmarks its facilities in the UK with 11 continental sites. It measures customer satisfaction and chalet occupation. When one unit shows a significantly better performance, the others learn how this was achieved.

Competitive

The second type of benchmarking is against direct competitors. This is often easier, however, for larger industries than smaller ones. It is also sometimes difficult to collect competitive information, although independent industry surveys and reports, if available, do offer insightful information.

ICL benchmarks more than 20 of its competitors both on company performance and on product technology. The information it gleans is distributed throughout the company to ensure that every function is aware of how it compares. On the overall performance side, information collected includes:

■ average debtors/creditors as a percentage of revenue;

■ research and development as a percentage of revenue;

■ return on capital employed; *and*

■ revenue per head.

On the product side, benchmarking at ICL includes:

■ Technology:

- how each component in a competitor's products compares with ICL's standards; *and*
- how quickly the competitor has assimilated new technology reliability.

■ Delivery:

- speed and reliability; *and*
- payment arrangements.

■ A variety of measurements in packaging, manufacturing, components costing and similar areas.[2]

Non competitive

It is possible to benchmark a process by measuring and comparing:

■ a related process in a non-competitive organisation;

■ a related process in a different industry; *and*

■ an unrelated process in a different industry.

In this way, improvements can be identified which can be adapted to the organisation.

Take the example of the BAA, which administers seven British airports. In addition to benchmarking itself against foreign airports, it has learned from companies in similar industries with similar problems, for example, Wembley Stadium and Ascot racecourse. All of these organisations must move, park and feed thousands of people in a confined space within a short period.

Best practice/world class

This approach to benchmarking involves learning from best practice or world-class organisations – the leaders of the process being benchmarked.

The Rover Group recognises the opportunities gained by looking outside at world-class practices in all fields to expand the organisation's vision of what is possible.

The need for benchmarking, prevalent throughout Rover, has been highlighted by a number of factors, including the increasingly competitive world market and the introduction of Japanese car plants across Europe.

All of Rover's business units have a requirement written into their business plans to benchmark their key processes. Management involvement is crucial in pushing for action on any measurements revealing improvement opportunities, and in removing blockages to improvement.

Rover Body and Pressings were chosen to pilot the process, and from their experience trainers have been developed to cascade the technique into the other business units.

Chris Millard, Logistics Director at the plant, recognises that to have a clear focus is vital: 'If you only benchmark an operation in total terms, you will miss. You examine and establish benchmarks for the processes which are the drive in achieving the targets set for the overall operation.'[3]

THE PITFALLS

Benchmarking is used most often to create a climate for change and to bring about continuous improvement. However, statistics show that nearly 70 per cent of all process improvement initiatives fail. The most common reasons for failure are:

■ lack of focus and priority;

■ lack of strategic relevance;

■ lack of leadership;

■ lack of perseverance; *and*

■ lack of planning.

Before an organisation begins a benchmarking programme, therefore, it is important to recognise the most typical causes or obstacles preventing the smooth and fast completion of the review.

Typical blockages include:

■ Management not 'buying into' the idea.

■ No clear 'owner' of the programme.

■ Failure to consider customer requirements.

■ Change of sponsor before completion of the programme.

■ Programme taking too long; loss of interest.

■ Not involving 'right' staff in the programme.

■ Team not measuring issues it agreed to address.

■ Programme causing too much disruption of work; not seen as relevant to work.

■ Conflicting objectives of the organisation and those of its benchmarking partners.

As we will see in subsequent chapters, careful preparation is the key to effective benchmarking programmes. Awareness of potential pitfalls is an important step in the process.

SUMMARY

■ This chapter provides a definition of benchmarking. It explains why in an increasingly competitive environment, benchmarking can be a powerful tool for change.

■ It describes the development of benchmarking as a management tool from the 1950s until today.

■ An overview is provided of the steps to effective benchmarking and the types of benchmarking that can be undertaken.

■ Finally, this chapter addresses the potential pitfalls in developing a benchmarking programme.

CHECKLIST

Use this checklist to help you plan how to put the key points from the chapter to use within your organisation.

1. Write down the reasons your organisation wishes to undertake a benchmarking programme and the benefits it hopes to gain from it. .

2. Describe the types of benchmarking you wish to undertake.

3. Identify the potential pitfalls or barriers you may encounter in developing a benchmarking programme.

4. Prepare a plan of action for ensuring the successful outcome of a benchmarking programme.

REFERENCES

1. DTI Publications, *Managing into the '90s: Best Practice Benchmarking.*

2. DTI Publications, *Managing into the '90s: Best Practice Benchmarking.*

3. DTI Publications, *Managing into the '90s: Best Practice Benchmarking.*

2

Preparing for benchmarking

In those companies who have adopted benchmarking effectively, it has become an everyday activity, part of the normal routine of day to day management. This is often due to the careful preparation that has taken place at the inception of the benchmarking process. It is said by many benchmarking practitioners that the outcome of the benchmarking process is only as good as the preparation which has gone into the process. It is also due to a disciplined approach being adopted to benchmarking within an organisational environment which is receptive to continuous improvement.

COMMON MISCONCEPTIONS ABOUT BENCHMARKING

Every manager has a responsibility to seek continually to improve the operations he or she controls. What frequently stops them is simple lack of knowledge – not knowing how much better he or she could be doing. It is human nature, without something to measure up against, to assume that current performance is near enough as good as you can get. Benchmarking leaves no room for such complacency.

For example, a factory supervisor was proud at having an unplanned downtime of only two hours a week on his manufacturing line. This was far and away the best performance of any of the three workshops on the site. Then he made an overseas visit and saw a company with a similar operation, which had reduced unplanned downtime to less than 30 minutes. Though not all the practices of the other firm were transferable, once he knew that 30 minutes was achievable, he and his engineers were able to devise their own ways to match and even improve on a standard he had previously thought impossible.

Such stories are not uncommon. You may have similar examples in your own company. Even then, how do you know the operation you compared with is truly the best, or are there superior performers elsewhere? And are you systematically comparing against the best on all the activities that are important to your business?

The art of cloning

Benchmarking is not a hit or miss process. Neither does it bring long-lasting effects when it is seen as a one-off event or activity that can be started and stopped at whim.

Furthermore, benchmarking does not mean cloning without thought, the success of other companies. What is best practice in one organisation cannot readily be transferred to another without a thorough understanding of the learning that has gone into achieving the standard, and recognition of the impact of the process on the culture of the organisation, in terms of both customer and employee reactions.

A UK office equipment supplier, for example, undertook a benchmarking exercise to identify best practice in telephone ordering processes. It established that an American company used a highly sophisticated automated telephone ordering system which was heralded by its customers for the speed and efficiency of its operation.

When the UK company adopted this standard in the

UK, the reaction of its own customers was one of horror. The system was seen to be impersonal and too American in its approach. Customers felt uncomfortable with the new ordering method and very soon the company had to revert to its former process.

Industrial tourism

A further misconception is that benchmarking is industrial tourism, that it consists of a series of costly and lengthy site visits. In fact as we will see later, the majority of the benchmarking process can take place from your own organisation. It does not have to be a costly exercise and it can be completed relatively quickly. Three to six months is the average time spent on a benchmarking project.

Measurement for measurement's sake

Benchmarking is not measurement for measurement's sake. There is a general resistance to being measured in many organisations, seen for example in the difficulties some organisations experience in introducing performance related pay.

Benchmarking goes further than merely making comparisons with competitors. It provides meaningful data on potential areas for improvement and, importantly, how these can be achieved.

Benchmarking is not appropriate for our organisation

Any aspect of an organisation can be benchmarked. It is a misconception that businesses cannot learn from others: 'it won't work unless it's invented here' is no longer relevant in an environment of increasing competition. The growth of many Japanese markets has been built on European and American complacency.

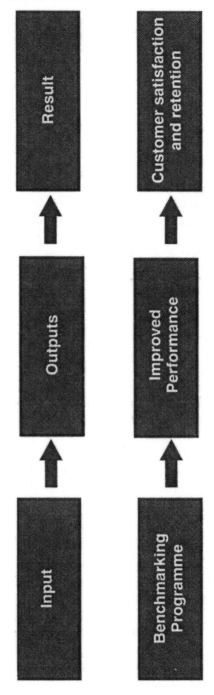

Figure 2.1 *Outcome of the benchmarking process*

If a benchmarking exercise is to be successful, it must increase awareness of what an organisation does well and what needs to change and why. Benchmarking exercises which measure cost alone invariably prove least successful.

A SYSTEMATIC APPROACH

Successful benchmarking involves a systematic and measured approach. This comprises a series of activities which enable managers to identify where improvement is needed to business performance and how these may be achieved.

Benchmarking involves establishing what makes the difference in customers' eyes between an ordinary supplier and an excellent one, finding out what is the 'best' that can be found and setting standards to deliver and exceed best practice.

However, enhanced business performance will only be achieved if the organisation is prepared and committed to change and if the objectives of the benchmarking process are clear and consistent with corporate goals.

Reasons for benchmarking

There may be a number of reasons why organisations adopt a benchmarking programme as a catalyst for change: It could be to:

■ increase efficiency;

■ create customer awareness;

■ enhance customer satisfaction;

■ improve profitability;

■ promote understanding;

■ make continuous improvements; *and*

■ gain commitment to corporate goals.

It is vital, upon embarking on a benchmarking project, therefore, that the objectives of the programme are clearly stated and that results can be measured.

British Rail Network South East, for example, undertook a benchmarking exercise to improve the standard of cleanliness on its trains. Customer satisfaction surveys demonstrated that, after punctuality, cleanliness is most important to customers. Through undertaking a best practice survey, British Rail Network South East was able to establish ways of improving its cleaning process. It identified British Airways as 'best in class' as it takes a team of 11 people nine minutes to clean a 250-seat Jumbo. Using the lessons learnt from British Airways and others, it applied these to the cleaning process for its 660-seat trains – which it now takes a team of ten eight minutes to clean.

BENCHMARKING AS A VEHICLE FOR CHANGE

Benchmarking plays a key role in many change programmes:

Benchmarking and total quality management

Benchmarking programmes often take place as part of total quality management initiatives. ICL, for example, first produced an internal guide on benchmarking as part of their quality programme in 1989.

Total quality management is a long-term commitment to satisfying customer requirements in every aspect of business operations. It is a philosophy which has been adopted by many organisations who wish to enhance customer satisfaction and thereby increase market share.

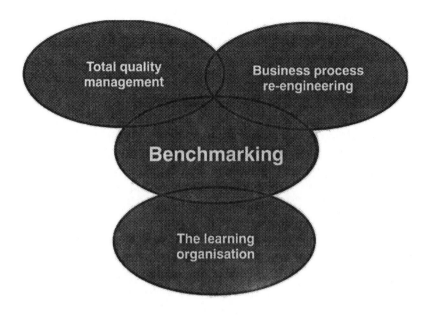

Figure 2.2 *Benchmarking in relation to change programmes*

The basic principle is that individuals are responsible for improving the service they provide their customers, be it external customers (outside the organisation) or internal customers (inside the organisation).

Companies who adopt a TQM approach make a commitment to continuous improvement. Often a team approach is adopted under the TQM banner to identify areas for improvement, generate and implement solutions. Increasingly, benchmarking is being adopted by organisations who are striving for continuous improvement because it offers an external perspective in the quest for service quality.

Customer satisfaction, therefore, is often a major benefit to be gained from benchmarking as it allows organisations to adopt 'helicopter vision' and helps prevent complacency through developing the discipline of focusing externally.

Benchmarking and process improvement

Benchmarking is only one tool in an armoury of techniques which can help improve business processes. Under the current fashion for Business Process Re-engineering, led by management consultants such as Hammer and Champy, benchmarking is being promoted as a process management tool.

Benchmarking exposes organisations to state-of-the-art practices, thereby acting as a catalyst for improvements in performance through emulations of best practice.

As we will see in later chapters, effective benchmarking cannot take place unless the organisations' existing processes are well understood. Benchmarking and process improvement are therefore fundamentally linked.

Benchmarking and the learning organisation

Benchmarking is a useful vehicle for learning. It causes individuals to assess their own performance and that of the organisation while, at the same time, encouraging involvement and creativity. Benchmarking is also an extremely powerful agent in the empowerment process as it encourages individuals to take responsibility for improvements. The life assurance company, Sun Life, adopted this route when it wished to increase the level of empowerment among its employees. A project team was formed to investigate best practice among leading organisations who have devolved responsibility to employees closest to the customer. Information was gathered on the different approaches to empowerment. This review assisted Sun Life in its assessment of its own levels of empowerment and the development of an action plan for change.

In Japan, benchmarking is so embedded into the culture that the term 'benchmarking' does not specifically exist as a word. Daitorsu (striving for the best in everything you do) and Shukko (seconding people to areas outside the organisation to learn and bring back new knowledge) sum up the principles of benchmarking in Japan which is linked to the concept of continuous learning.

Requirements for implementation

Measuring and studying the way a company works often reveals and quantifies unknown weaknesses which can boost the argument for change. In order for benchmarking to be implemented successfully, organisations must address the following requirements:

1. The need for senior management commitment to the project. Commitment also to act on any major opportunities for improvement that are revealed.

2. Commitment to the resources necessary to undertake the benchmarking programme (mainly people and time).

3. Training for employees who will have to gather in information needed to identify and analyse best practice.

Of these the most critical is senior management commitment. To prevent benchmarking becoming an academic exercise with no relevance to the business, senior management must own the process and be seen to guide and support the programme.

PREPARING FOR THE BENCHMARKING PROJECT

There are five steps in the planning process in preparation for benchmarking:

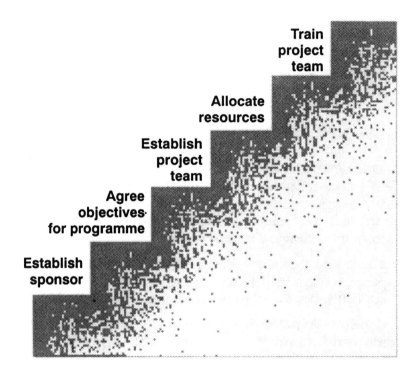

Figure 2.3 *Benchmarking – five planning steps*

1. Establish a sponsor

Before a benchmarking initiative is undertaken, a 'sponsor' or 'champion' of the process must be established. This person must be sufficiently senior within the organisation to drive the project through and to support the findings of the benchmarking exercise.

Importantly the 'sponsor' needs to be familiar with the process under review and be desirous of the need for change.

A sponsor has a vital role to play in linking the overall vision of where the organisation is heading to the task of the benchmarking team. In this way benchmarking can be put into the context of organisational goals. This helps to create a focus for project team members.

2. Agree objectives for the programme – with time frames

As stated earlier, it is useful to be as clear as possible about the objectives of the benchmarking project. It is also helpful to remember the intangible objectives of the programme, such as increased teamwork and understanding, as well as the tangible outcomes.

In addition, time frames should always be set, as frameworks, for a benchmarking programme. This establishes parameters in which the project team can operate.

3. Establish a project team

Success of a benchmarking project largely depends on the care that is taken in selecting the appropriate project team members for the task and in training and supporting them.

Surveys of top-performing US firms like Xerox, Motorola and AT&T suggest that the effectiveness of benchmarking activities is underpinned by the successful selection and development of team members.

Having gained commitment and a sponsor for the project, the next step is to form a project team headed by a project team leader. Ideally this person should be the process owner – the person who has ultimate responsibility for the outcome of the process. Alternatively the leader should be actively involved in the process to be benchmarked.

· Team members should have sufficient clout and credibility to get their recommendations approved, otherwise their efforts will fail. Members should be drawn from across the organisation. The team should ideally consist of five to eight people. Any less than this number and the team will find it difficult to operate. Any more and meetings become protracted unless a very strong approach is taken by the project leader.

Participants should have the knowledge/influence/capacity to undertake the programme. Ideally, the mix of team members should include those who are:

■ good communicators;

■ good motivators;

■ prepared to question and challenge the status quo;

■ systematic and analytical in their approach;

■ creative in their outlook;

■ willing to progress the task in their own time, outside team meetings;

■ able to promote good team spirit;

■ willing to achieve the task; *and*

■ credible within the organisation.

It is beneficial to ensure the team consists of both managers and staff who are both users and customers of the process which is under review. The team should include a mix of seniority and knowledge.

When BP Chemicals' Hull manufacturing and research site conducted an in-depth benchmarking study into best practice in human resource management, it set up a team of six people. Four of the team came from HR and two from manufacturing. The team comprised a balance of 'old hands' and 'young blood'. Two people had also been members of the manufacturing bench-marking team to ensure continuity.

Whatever the team composition, it should be headed by a project leader who can coordinate the activities of the group and ensure that there are the resources to complete the project.

At the initial meeting, the project leader needs to ensure that the team understands the objective of the project and is working to a common aim. Also timescales should be established both for the project as a whole and for the project team meetings.

The project team leader may choose to chair the meetings, or, as an alternative, the role of chair may be undertaken on a rotational basis. Whoever takes on the role of chair should ensure that responsibility is allocated for tasks and that these are worked through. The project team leader may also need to ensure the smooth liaison with outside experts and other parts of the organisation.

Invariably it will take some time before the dynamics of the project team ensure good working practices.

Many teams go through a 'storming' phase where disagreements and conflict surface. Although this can be uncomfortable, challenge is healthy in a team. Team members should be encouraged to 'think out of the box' and question existing working practices.

4. Allocate resources

Once project team members have been established, it is prudent to ensure that the time has been allocated to them to undertake the project. Benchmarking does not have to be a costly exercise in terms of purchases; it is time and people which are the biggest outlays.

A helpful tip is to schedule time in team members' diaries at the beginning of the project. Likewise, team

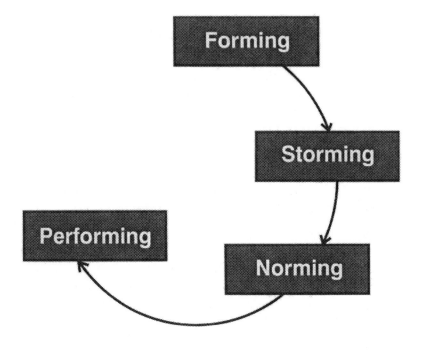

Figure 2.4 *The four phases of team development*
Source: Bruce Tuckman, 1965

members should establish the importance of the project with their managers and colleagues so that the review does not suffer at a later date through a conflict of priorities.

5. Train the project team

It is a fallacy to believe that a benchmarking project team does not require training. Team members often need training in four discrete areas:

1. the benchmarking process;

2. research techniques;

3. data analysis; *and*

4. team working.

■ **The benchmarking process**

Team members will benefit from an in-depth understanding of the stages of the process and what is involved in each. Here it is often useful to include relevant experience of people who have been involved in benchmarking studies in the past.

■ **Research techniques**

Whether the study is conducted internally or externally, project team members will need to be skilled in designing and conducting research, be it via questionnaires, face to face interviews or telephone surveys.

■ **Data analysis**

Likewise, once the information has been collated, there are a variety of tools which can be used for data analysis. It is helpful and more cost effective for project team members to be able to conduct the analysis. Training can also be provided in this area.

■ **Team working**

As some of the benchmarking team members may not have experience of working together as a team, it can often be helpful to hold a team-building event prior to the beginning of the benchmarking study. Included in this event can be guidelines on how to form an effective team.

SUMMARY

■ This chapter sets out the steps that need to be taken in preparation for the benchmarking process.

- It dispels some common misconceptions about benchmarking and advocates a systematic approach to benchmarking studies. It describes the need for clear objectives at the inception of the project.

- The links to total quality management and process improvement through benchmarking are discussed, as are the opportunities benchmarking brings to the 'learning organisation'.

- One of the most important requirements for implementation of a successful benchmarking project is the commitment of senior management.

- Finally, a five-step plan for benchmarking is described.

CHECKLIST

Use this checklist to help you plan how to put the key points from the chapter into use within your organisation.

1. Hold a series of 'education' events in your organisation to familiarise managers with the benchmarking concept.

2. Establish a set of objectives for a benchmarking study.

3. Identify the links between benchmarking and others of your organisation's change programmes such as total quality management, process improvement or initiatives for learning.

4. Identify a sponsor for the programme (ideally someone in senior management who is committed to the need for change).

5. Form a project team, elect a leader and train project team members.

6. Agree a timetable for the project and diary dates.

7. Agree the roles and responsibilities of the project team members.

3

Overview of the benchmarking process

Having put in place the stepping stones to prepare for benchmarking you will now be in a position to undertake the benchmarking study. This requires a systematic approach involving six stages:

1. Identify and understand your processes.

2. Agree what and who to benchmark.

3. Collect data.

4. Analyse data and identify gaps.

5. Plan and action improvements.

6. Review.

There are a number of variations which some companies have adopted on this six-step approach, but most follow the Deming principle (Figure 3.1) which is often applied to total quality initiatives.

A SYSTEMATIC APPROACH

Each stage in the six-step approach needs to be completed

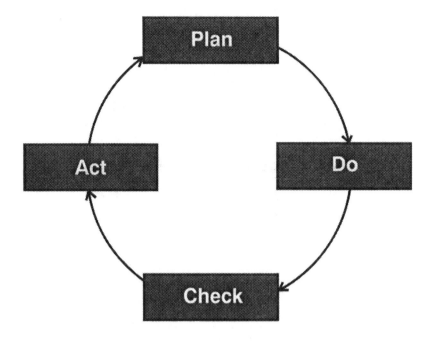

Figure 3.1 *The Deming PDCA cycle*

before moving to the next. Stages one and two 'Identifying and understanding your processes' and 'Agreeing what and who to benchmark' will probably take the longest time for the project team to complete.

These stages together with stages three and four – 'Collect data' and 'Analyse data and identify gaps' – can often be completed within a few months' duration. Stages five and six – 'Action' and 'Review' – may well take longer to implement depending on the benchmarking exercise.

Once agreement has been reached to begin a benchmarking study and a project team has been formed, an outline of the steps involved in each stage of the benchmarking study is as follows:

1. Identify and understand your processes

This stage involves gaining an in-depth knowledge of the organisation's processes in order fully to understand its operation and the key factors which determine its success.

This stage is critical to the effective outcome of the benchmarking project as unless a careful analysis has been undertaken of the organisation's chosen process prior to selecting benchmarking partners, the project team will not be in a position to select the right partners nor gather the correct data.

2. Agree what and who to benchmark

The project team may already have a perception of potential benchmarking partners. However, intuition needs to be supplemented with detailed knowledge. It is important at this stage of the benchmarking process clearly to identify what and who to benchmark through careful analysis of the options available. This stage also involves the team in identifying how best to collect the data.

3. Collect data

There are a variety of methods for collecting data from benchmarking partners. This can come about through the direct exchange of information or through desk research. However the information is gathered, its quality will directly reflect the appropriateness of the questions asked.

4. Analyse data and identify gaps

Once data has been collated, both quantitatively and qualitatively, it is possible to establish best practice and identify the gaps between the organisation's performance and the performance of the benchmarking partners who provide the highest standards. In this way differences can be established and a plan of action for improvement developed.

5. Plan and action improvements

The action-planning stage of the benchmarking process involves generating ideas on how improvements can be made and putting forward ideas for implementation. The communication of the results of the benchmarking exercise to other parts of the organisation (and benchmarking partners where possible) so they are aware of the need for change is critical.

The project team needs to define clearly the changes which need to take place in order to reach and exceed the benchmarks which have been established as part of the programme. The team will also be responsible for introducing the improvements into the organisation and for ensuring their smooth implementation.

6. Review

The benchmarking process is iterative. At each stage of the study progress should be reviewed and the next steps adjusted in the light of the findings. For example, after completing stage 3, the collection of data, it may turn out that further information is required from benchmarking partners or that other criteria need to be assessed or further benchmarking partners found.

In addition, after the 'plan and action improvement' stage, progress should be monitored and reviewed.

As the pace of change increases dramatically in the commercial world so best practice will change. The process of undertaking benchmarking should be never-ending and part of the culture of continuous improvement.

Examples of systematic approach

Organisations who have several years' experience of undertaking benchmarking studies usually develop their own framework for the benchmarking process.

Digital Equipment Company, for example, has developed a four-step approach to benchmarking:

1. What to benchmark.

2. How is it done at Digital?

3. Who is the best?

4. How do they do it?

Royal Mail sees benchmarking as a valuable tool in achieving its declared mission to be recognised as the world's best distributor of text and packages.

The quality department at Royal Mail developed materials to help benchmark teams, based on a well researched and defined process.

The clarity in defining how the benchmarking process works has helped Royal Mail communicate the value of it and involve all staff in implementing it. An example of how the awareness of benchmarking has cascaded throughout the culture can be seen in a benchmarking exercise recently started within the marketing department. Brought together at a departmental conference, a team of benchmarking volunteers is working through the process. The team, who are being given special training, is made up of a mixture of functions within the marketing department, giving a variety of perspectives.

The team decided to focus on aspects of product development, including the management of consultants and internal communications. It found that best practice in product development transfers easily between industries, opening up the opportunity for a wide spread of benchmarking partners. One over-riding criterion it imposed in selecting partners was that they should share a total quality focus. This criterion has been built into Royal Mail's benchmarking process.[1]

SUMMARY

- This chapter provides an overview of the six stages in a systematic approach to benchmarking.

- It outlines an example of one company's approach to benchmarking.

CHECKLIST

Use this checklist to help you plan how to put the key points from the chapter to use with your organisation.

1. Become familiar with each phase in the benchmarking process.

2. Agree the detailed steps in each part of the benchmarking process with the project team.

3. Describe the activities in each phase and decide who will be responsible for them.

REFERENCES

1. DTI Publications, *Managing into the '90s: Best Practice Benchmarking.*

4

Step 1: Identify and understand your processes

It is helpful to begin a benchmarking programme on a small scale so that the organisation can gain lessons from the systematic approach that is adopted. The lessons can then be applied to other parts of the business. In this way the cost of benchmarking can be kept to a minimum as benchmarking can take place on a process by process basis.

UNDERSTAND YOUR PROCESSES

The preparation stage of benchmarking is the most critical. Until an organisation understands its business processes it is difficult to compare them with other parts of the organisation, or with external sources.

Identifying processes

Everything which happens in a company is part of a process. All processes should lead to achievement of an organisation's aims.

The first question, therefore, to ask is: 'What is the

organisation in business for?'. It is easy to recognise that Disney, for example, sees itself in the entertainment business. If you run a restaurant or a pub you may have a different outlook on what business you are in. The licence trade? The catering business? Taking a broader outlook, any pub or restaurant is in the entertainment business too. Their aim is to satisfy their guests by ensuring they have a good experience in their restaurant or pub and that they want to return. In this way outlets not only attract but retain customers. The focus of all the processes that support an organisation's business operation is to achieve this aim.

A process is a series of steps or sequence of activities, the end result of which is to achieve client satisfaction, ie providing what the customer needs, when they need it and as they expect it.

Here for example is a description of five of the 33 groups of processes which Mercury, the telecommunication company, have identified:

■ The delivery of telephone services to a new customer.

■ The development of new products and services to the future requirements of customers.

■ The management of material supplies to ensure network capacity is available as required.

■ The billing of customers to give information on use of services which the customer requires, as well as to collect revenue.

■ The communication with employees using communication processes.

Processes should be customer driven

The result of all processes should be to satisfy a customer requirement. A customer may be internal or external. The

46

customer is the person who receives the output or benefits from the process.

Identify added value processes

The concept of a value chain can help organisations identify the various processes within an organisation which offer value to both the internal or external customer. It is useful to map out an organisation's process to identify critical success factors.

Digital Equipment Company has developed a checklist for identifying crucial business processes which are fundamental to the organisation's success. For each process they ask:

- Is the process critical to achieving customer satisfaction?

- Is the process critical to the organisation's ability to survive and flourish?

Benchmarking studies make a measurable impact on the bottom line when they bring about improvements to core processes. Processes can be divided into those which are primary processes. Primary processes are directly concerned with delivering a product or service to the external customer. Secondary processes support the primary processes within an organisation and are often concerned with providing a service to the internal customer.

Figure 4.1 gives an example of a value chain demonstrating primary and support processes for a manufacturing company.

Ask your customers

Organisations need to identify which of their primary processes or core activities are critical for the company to

Structure of firm (general management, planning, finance, etc)				
Human resource management (recruitment, training, development, etc)				
Research & development (product and process)				
Procurement (function of purchasing inputs)				
Inbound logistics (receiving, storing materials, handling, etc)	Operations (machining, packaging, assembly, etc)	Outbound logistics (storing, distribution, vehicle operations)	Marketing and sales (advertising, promotions, sales, etc)	Service (installations, repair, parts supply etc)

Support processes

Primary processes

Figure 4.1 *Value chain for a manufacturing company*

48

remain in business and to be successful. Customers will have a clear idea of what is important to them. A useful starting point is to ask them:

- What are we good at?
- What areas do we need to improve?

An engineering company, for example, carried out a survey among its customers to identify which processes were really important to them and where they could improve. It discovered that fast delivery of technically proven products was important but where improvements really needed to be made was in the organisation's customer service process.

Digital's approach to process improvement, in which benchmarking plays an important role, focuses on customer requirements (Figure 4.2).

Ask your employees

People working within the organisation will also have opinions on the processes within which they are working. Often the quality of service that is provided within an organisation has a direct effect on the quality of service that is provided to external customers.

Employee attitude surveys, focus groups and in-depth interviews can provide useful feedback on how relationships within the organisation can be improved.

Ask employees to identify factors which they perceive as critical to your success in your company and what they perceive has the biggest influence on your company's performance. Compare the responses of your employees to those of your customers.

Ask your suppliers

A further input in understanding your core processes is to gain feedback from your suppliers. People who work

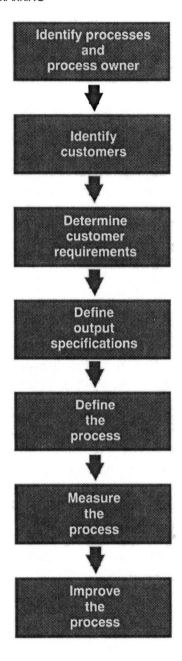

Figure 4.2 *The Digital approach to process improvement*

with the organisation, yet who can also take an external perspective, can prove to be an invaluable source of information.

PLOT OUT YOUR PROCESS, PEEL BACK THE LAYERS

Once you have begun to identify the core processes in your organisation you can map out where each process links into others.

On the surface, what appears to be a single process is made up of a series of activities which become more complex as you peel away the layers to discover secondary and tertiary processes which support the primary process. Hewlett Packard call this the 'Onion Factor', Rover has termed this 'the Virtuous Circle'.

The concept is one of a hierarchy of processes. If we take human resource management as a process, for example, we see that human resource management is the primary process; peeling away the covering layer, underneath lie the secondary processes such as:

■ recruitment and selection;

■ training and development;

■ compensation and benefits;

■ employee communication; *and*

■ succession planning.

Each secondary process in turn serves as an umbrella for tertiary processes, and so on until all the layers of the onion have been peeled away.

Xerox Corporation, for example, has identified and mapped out ten primary level processes for its business as a whole and 57 secondary level processes. It designates a numeric to each of the processes that it benchmarks so that there is a common understanding of where the process stands in the hierarchy.

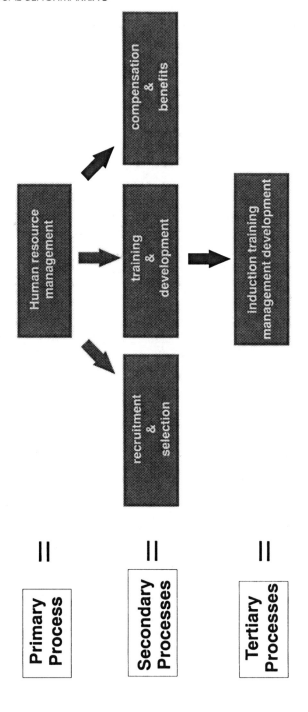

Figure 4.3 *The hierarchy of processes for human resource management*

Analysing the process

Analysing and understanding the process in all its shapes and forms is crucial to the success of a benchmarking study. Project team members need to understand the activities that make up the process and the relationship of the process with other parts of the business.

Every process has an input and output (Figure 4.4). Outputs should be measurable and customer driven, for example:

■ Delivery made on time and to customers' satisfaction.

■ Employees trained in the ten requirements of health and safety regulations.

Figure 4.4 *A process input and output*

CHARTING THE PROCESS

Charting the process on a step by step basis helps increase understanding of each of the activities. It helps to 'brainstorm' the different steps. One means of achieving this is to 'mind map' the process.

Mind mapping

Mind mapping is a form of brainstorming which encourages free-wheeling. It is highly participative in its approach. Mind mapping is best carried out with the use of 'Post It' type notes which can be taken off the page andordered into a sequence once the initial brainstorm has taken place.

A TEN-POINT CHECKLIST

For each process it should be possible to identify:

1. What is the output of the process? (in measurable terms)

2. Who is the customer? (the recipient of the output)

3. What are the customers' requirements? (eg quality, timing, cost.)

4. Who is the process owner? (the person ultimately responsible for ensuring the process meets customer requirements)

5. How does the process work? (what are the start and end points?)

6. What is involved in the process? (the activities or steps of the process)

7. Who is involved? (individuals, departments, suppliers)

8. When do things happen? (time scales, elapsed time)

9. How much does it cost? (in terms of time, money and people)

10. What are the problems with the existing process? (as perceived by the process owner, those involved and customers)

As a first step in understanding the process, project team members should brainstorm the responses to all of these questions.

To begin mind mapping the process take a large piece of paper. Hand everyone in the team a set of sticky notes and pens. Draw a circle in the centre of the large piece of paper and write the name of the process in the circle as a reminder.

Next, encourage team members to think of activities involved in the process and write these on the sticky

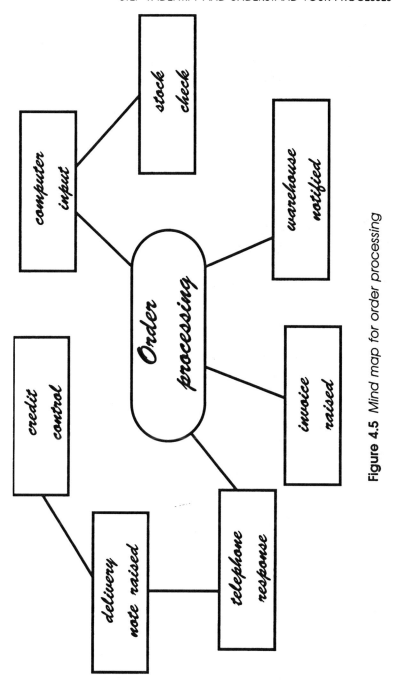

Figure 4.5 Mind map for order processing

notes. They should then place the notes on the large piece of paper, linking them via lines to the central circle and indicating relationships by drawing lines to link activities.

This method allows team members quickly to identify different stages of the process before ordering the sticky notes into a sequence of activities.

Fishbone diagram*

An alternative and more structured approach to mind mapping involves brainstorming activities in the process and grouping them together under headings or boxes using the outline of a fish skeleton as a framework. This provides a visual vehicle for demonstrating the inter-relationships between steps in the process. It shows the process as a whole while at the same time it dissects the sections.

To draw a fishbone diagram:

1. Take a large piece of paper and give all team members a pen.

2. Draw a fish shape (head and skeleton) on the paper.

3. Write the name of the process in the head of the fish.

4. Thinking of the different activities in the process, label each bone with the name of each major activity (or sub process).

5. From each of the bones draw smaller bones to identify activities which occur in the sub process.

Process flow diagrams

An alternative approach is to prepare diagrams showing the flow of the process. This is particularly helpful where

---

*The fishbone diagram was developed by Professor Ishikawa

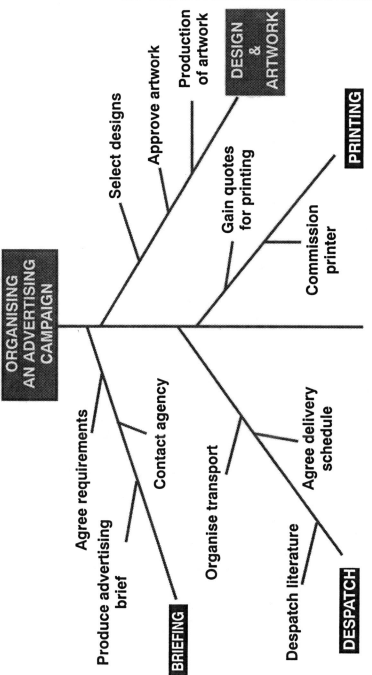

Figure 4.6 Fishbone diagram for organising an advertising campaign

57

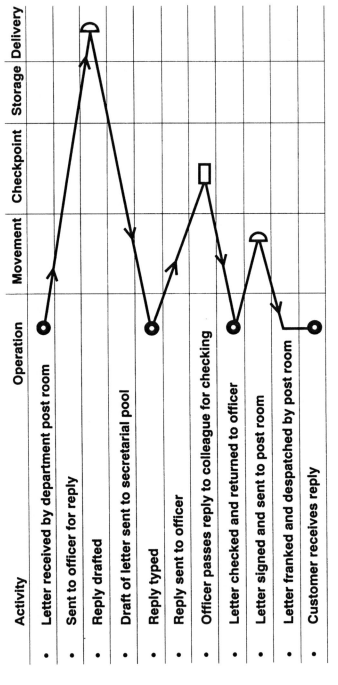

Figure 4.7 Process flow diagram for Government Department

a single item is handled/moved through a number of stages. There are five categories which are used to symbolise activity:

1. ○ Operation – the main activities in the process.

2. ↓ Movement – of product/people/items etc.

3. ☐ Quality or quantity checkpoint.

4. ▽ Storage, eg filing.

5. D Delay or hold up between activities.

Figure 4.7 shows a flow diagram for the fictitious process of replying to a letter sent to a Government Department.

Using this method it is possible therefore to identify the blockages involved in the process because of storage or delay.

Time elapsed diagram

An alternative flow diagram charts the time elapsed from the inception of the process to its outcome. A time elapsed diagram for the Government Department would look like Figure 4.8.

In this way it is possible not only to identify the sequence of activities in a process but also where significant time delays occur.

Process mapping

Many businesses find that it is helpful to map out each activity in a process using a set of conventional and proven mapping symbols. This can be particularly useful when project teams are dealing with complex activities which it would otherwise be difficult to describe. The graphic display of the process can also prove invaluable when making comparison with benchmarking partners.

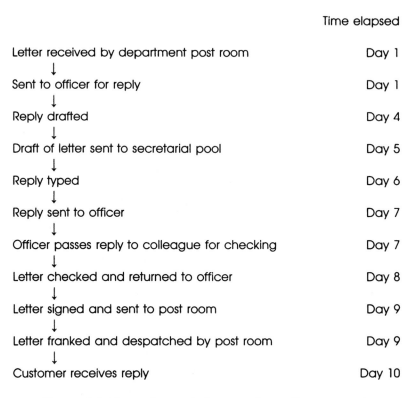

Time elapsed

Letter received by department post room	Day 1
↓	
Sent to officer for reply	Day 1
↓	
Reply drafted	Day 4
↓	
Draft of letter sent to secretarial pool	Day 5
↓	
Reply typed	Day 6
↓	
Reply sent to officer	Day 7
↓	
Officer passes reply to colleague for checking	Day 7
↓	
Letter checked and returned to officer	Day 8
↓	
Letter signed and sent to post room	Day 9
↓	
Letter franked and despatched by post room	Day 9
↓	
Customer receives reply	Day 10

Figure 4.8 *Time elapsed diagram for a Government Department's response to a customer letter*

It can also be used as a means of understanding areas for potential improvements before a benchmarking study begins.

The symbols used in process mapping are:

⟶ process flow

▢ activity steps

◯ start

▢ end

◇ decision point

▱ information block

Figure 4.9 shows a process flow for a help line responsible for fixing internal faults.

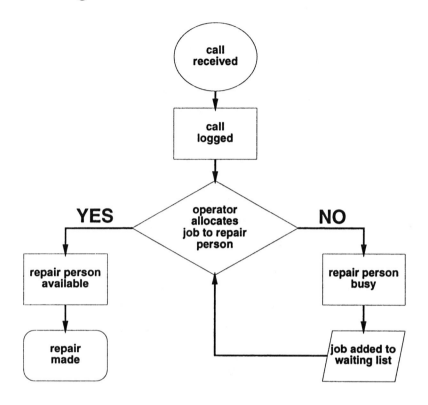

Figure 4.9 *Process flow diagram for an internal repair help line*

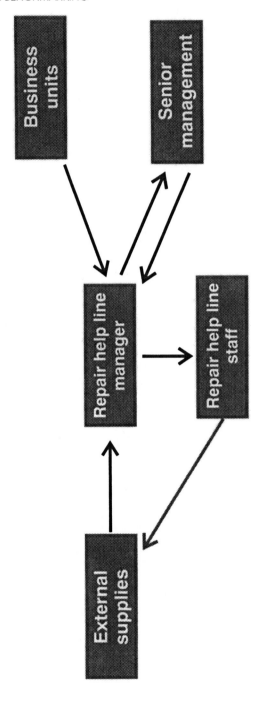

Figure 4.10 *An information flow diagram*

There are a number of computer-based packages available which will provide a template for process mapping.

Information flow diagrams

A further mapping technique is the information flow diagram. This can be used to understand and clarify the flow of information, thereby identifying what information is currently available and what information is missing in the process.

The flow of information between groups is analysed and the direction of information flow indicated via one-way or two-way arrows. The example in Figure 4.9, of the repair help line, could be reworked as an information flow diagram (Figure 4.10).

Figure 4.10 shows that the flow of information is two-way between the repair help line manager and senior managers and the business units and senior managers. However, there are information flow lapses in other areas.

Supply chain

When seeking to understand a process, the temptation is often to concentrate intensely on the activities within the process. However, the project team must not forget to take an external perspective. The team needs to consider the value chain for the organisation including the total sequence of events leading up to the delivery of the product or service to the end customer.

Recognising where the unit/department/organisation sits in the supply chain helps the team identify the importance of the process to the overall business. External suppliers can be included in the mapping too.

It may be, for example, that improving the relationships between different parts of the supply chain will produce

Figure 4.11 *Part of a supply chain for an estate agency*

greater benefits to the organisation than addressing in depth the activities within one process. Take the example of a group of valuers who are part of a large chain of estate agents. It may be more effective for the business to address the way parts of the supplier-chain react with each other, for example, than to conduct a benchmarking study into processes within the valuers' department. The same can be said of organisations with large amounts of external supplies.

Mapping out the organisation's supply chain helps establish the links between external or internal supplies and other part of the business (Figure 4.11).

MEASUREMENT OF PROCESSES

As an understanding is gained of an organisation's processes the project team needs to document the measures of performance which are in place for each step in the process. These performance indicators serve as in-house standards against which the project team can make comparisons with external benchmarking factors.

Metrics should be prepared for each process. These can encompass performance indicators such as cost, time, quantity, quality or people involvement (Figure 4.12).

INITIAL EFFORT BRINGS RETURNS

The initial phase of process understanding may seem to take time and effort, particularly when the temptation may be to move directly to contacting benchmarking partners and beginning a study.

Hewlett Packard adopted benchmarking as an essential part of their total quality approach. They, like many other organisations, have found that the most challenging aspect of benchmarking is gaining a thorough knowledge of the process which they are going to benchmark.

65

Activity	Cost	Time	Quantity	Quality	People involved
Call logged	£15	within 3 minutes	1	correct greeting	1
Job allocated	£25	within 30 minutes	1	customer details given	1
Repair undertaken	£55	2 hours	1	fixed first time	1

Figure 4.12 *Performance indicators for an internal faults line*

Understanding your processes is therefore a crucial step towards benchmarking success.

SUMMARY

■ Without a good understanding of your own organisation's business processes comparison cannot be made with benchmarking partners.

■ A process is a series of activities with an input and an output. The objectives of all processes should be to satisfy the customer.

■ It is beneficial to ask your customers, suppliers and employees what they perceive to be your organisation's key processes.

■ There are a variety of techniques for representing processes in a graphic format. These include recognising that there is a hierarchy or layer of processes beneath each process and plotting the activities in the process.

■ Fishbone diagrams, process flow diagrams, time elapsed diagrams, process mapping, information flow diagrams and supply chain mapping are tools which can be used to understand processes and which can provide a framework for comparison of data when benchmarking begins.

CHECKLIST

Use this checklist to help you plan how to put the key points from the chapter into use in your organisation.

1. Brainstorm a list of the processes in your organisation.

2. Consider what your company is in business for, identify the core processes which are crucial to your organisation's success.

3. Explore your customers', suppliers' and employees' perceptions of your processes and areas for improvement.

4. Use some of the charting techniques listed in the chapter to analyse your processes in more detail.

5. Use the ten-point checklist on page 54 to gather information on your processes.

6. Obtain information on the performance indicators currently used to measure your processes.

Step 2: Identify what and who to benchmark

As we have seen in Chapter 4, the organisations which gain most from benchmarking are those which have a clear idea of what they want to benchmark and why.

Every aspect of an organisation can be benchmarked including:

■ customer satisfaction;

■ speed of service;

■ human resource management;

■ internal communication; *and*

■ cash management.

The most effective benchmarking teams limit themselves to reviewing processes which are key success criteria for business performance and which are directly linked to the organisation's mission.

NCR, for example, used its organisation's 'vision and ten' mission statement to identify key success factors in its benchmarking programme. It supplemented these with interviews with all of its senior managers. In this way the project team was able to establish a checklist of twenty key measures against which it wished to benchmark itself. A database was completed for each. These included:

■ manufacturing cycle time;

■ on time supply and delivery;

■ shipment;

■ concept to market;

■ supplier delivery;

■ return on assets;

■ return on technical investment; *and*

■ revenue per employee.[1]

DECIDING WHAT TO BENCHMARK

One senior manager summed up a common problem in initiating a benchmarking programme: 'There are so many different areas where we believe that benchmarking can be applied, it is difficult to know where to begin'.

Even if a company has identified that a number of processes can be benchmarked, it is often difficult to establish in which order to begin a benchmarking project and which study will bring the greatest return.

One way to decide what to benchmark is to clarify what you hope to gain from the study. The first step is to identify processes of key importance to your business and what you hope to gain from a benchmarking exercise.

Most projects can be categorised as:

■ process benchmarking,

■ strategic benchmarking or

■ statistical benchmarking.

(Sometimes studies cover a combination of all three areas.)

It could be that you wish to make comparisons between your business processes and processes of other areas of your business or external organisations to establish best practice. For example, one Hospital Trust conducted a benchmarking study with organisations outside the Health Service to determine the best practice in appointment systems.

You may wish to benchmark strategically, in order, for example, to help create a strategy of differentiation. One computer hardware manufacturer undertook a wide-ranging study of best practice in customer service. The results of the study helped the company develop a competitive advantage through the design and implementation of a customer service strategy.

Statistical benchmarking is the third approach. Here, benchmarking partners make direct comparisons between one measure of performance within a process and another. For example, the number of people employed to undertake a certain task/the revenue per employee/the number of days training per employee, etc. (The danger of adopting only this quantitative approach is explained later in this chapter.)

Analytical Hierarchy Process

One way to select benchmarking topics is to adopt the route which Xerox and others advocate, called AHP – Analytical Hierarchy Process.

This method, which was developed by Thomas Saaty of the University of Pennsylvania, USA, provides a structure for the team to select the process to benchmark. It requires the project team to rank decision alternatives against a common set of decision criteria. In this way emotive decisions can be avoided.[2]

This is a five-step approach involving:

1. Developing a set of decision criteria to evaluate alternative processes;

71

2. Establishing through consensus the weighted value of the decision criteria;

3. Ranking the processes under consideration against each of the decision criteria;

4. Making a comparison of the scores for each process;

5. Selecting the most appropriate alternative.

A typical analysis using the AHP route would therefore be as follows.

Activity 1: Establish decision criteria

An example of decision criteria which the team has agreed would be:

■ Estimated time to complete study.

■ Current knowledge of process.

■ Availability of benchmarking partners.

■ Importance to organisational mission.

Activity 2: Establish weighted value of decision criteria

Each decision criteria is weighted and expressed as a percentage out of a total of 100. For example in the criteria established above the following values were given:

	Score (per cent)
■ Estimated time to complete study.	20
■ Current knowledge of process.	30
■ Availability of benchmarking partners.	15
■ Importance to organisational mission.	35
	100

Process	Time to complete (20%)	Knowledge of process (30%)	Availability of partners (15%)	Importance to mission (35%)
Customer satisfaction				
Human resource management				
Manufacturing cycle				
Cash management				

Figure 5.1 *A decision criteria table*

Activity 3: Ranking activities

The team constructs a table listing the alternative processes under consideration for benchmarking down the left hand side and the decision criteria across the top, as shown in Figure 5.1.

On a scale of 1 to 5 with 5 = very high and 1 = very low, each process is then ranked by the team to see how well it stands up against the business decision-making criteria.

A numerical value is given for each process against each criteria, as shown in Figure 5.2.

Activity 4: Making a comparison of the totals of each score

The score in each cell is then multiplied by the value of each decision criterion, as shown in Figure 5.3.

The scores for each process are then totalled; in this example, 60 + 90 + 60 + 175 = 385.

This activity is repeated for each of the processes so that a comparative score is achieved for each of the processes, shown in Figure 5.4.

Activity 5: Selecting the most appropriate alternative

The final activity involves selecting the most appropriate process to benchmark, based on the highest score.

Importance/urgency matrix

Another method of deciding which subject area to take is to use an importance/urgency matrix. Here project team members place each process on a matrix. One axis represents the importance of the process to the future success of the business. The second axis represents the urgency of improving the process (Figure 5.5).

The processes of high importance and high urgency are those which the project team need to tackle first.

Process	Time to complete (20%)	Knowledge of process (30%)	Availability of partners (15%)	Importance to mission (35%)
Customer satisfaction	3	3	4	5
Human resource management	2	3	3	4
etc. as categories in figure 5.1				

Figure 5.2 *Ranking of processes against decision criteria*

Process	Time to complete (20%)	Knowledge of process (30%)	Availability of partners (15%)	Importance to mission (35%)
Customer satisfaction	3 x 20 = 60	3 x 30 = 90	4 x 15 = 60	5 x 35 = 175
Human resource management	2 x 20 = 40	3 x 30 = 90	3 x 15 = 45	4 x 35 = 140
etc as categories in figure 5.1				

Figure 5.3 *Scoring*

	Total score	Rank
Customer satisfaction	385	1
Human resource management	315	3
Manufacturing cycle	355	2
Cash management	310	4

Figure 5.4 *Comparative scoring*

Problem checklist

A further method of identifying processes most in need of improvement is to make a selection of suitable processes and then to log problems arising as a result of the processes over a trial period. In this way quantitative data is made available to project team members to use to make a decision about which process to benchmark.

Above all, project team members should remember that items of strategic importance to the organisation provide higher potential for success.

WHO TO BENCHMARK AGAINST?

To benchmark successfully, care must be taken in the choice of partners. These are other business units who are prepared to co-operate in the exchange of information and learning points and who may expect reciprocal sharing from your organisation too.

There are four routes which are generally taken to establishing benchmarking partners:

1. To look inside the organisation.

2. To gather external data in other competitive businesses.

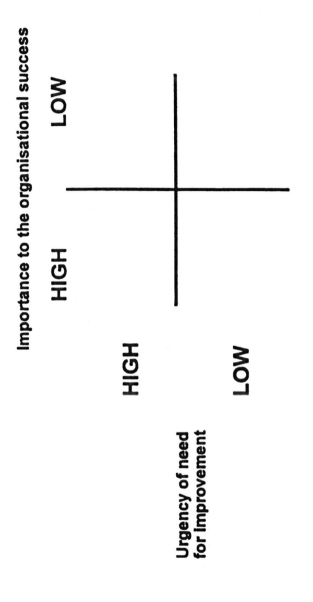

Figure 5.5 *Importance/urgency matrix*

3. To gather external data in the same industry or similar areas.

4. To establish partnerships with organisations who are considered 'world best' or 'best in class', irrespective of their industry sector or location.

Car manufacturers Rover have become benchmarking enthusiasts. Benchmarking studies take place in every aspect of their business. Not only do Rover benchmark against their competitors but they also review the practices of their suppliers and working partners such as Honda. They have also formed links with best practice companies such as IBM and British Airways.

Rover are so committed to benchmarking that they have developed their own internal database to which everyone in the company has access.

Like Rank Xerox, Rover find themselves as the target of other companies' benchmarking services since they are seen to be leaders in their field. Consequently both firms have begun to charge for their services.[3]

The route to adopt to partnering depends on the process to be benchmarked and the type of organisation. There are advantages and disadvantages to each route. Results in terms of improvements in performance, however, are directly related to the degree of external perception that is given to a benchmarking project.

Change can take two forms:

■ Incremental change which happens gradually over time; *and*

■ Step change which involves radical differences in working practices and procedures.

Best practice benchmarking brings about the highest potential improvement leaps and as such acts as a catalyst in step change processes.

Internal benchmarking

The advantages

There are relatively fewer problems in comparing internal benchmarks with external ones and it is often via this process that many organisations begin to benchmark.

The advantages of internal benchmarking are that it is easier to deal with partners who share a common language, culture and systems than to look outside the organisation. Access to data is normally easier, as benchmarking is generally perceived as a low-risk activity.

Benchmarking partners can be found within your own site or in different geographic locations, business units or group of companies.

As you will be sharing a common language and working practices and systems will often be the same, communication normally proves easy. Therefore an internal benchmarking study can be a good test-bed to pilot the benchmarking concept and the returns can be relatively quick.

The disadvantages

The major disadvantage of an internal benchmarking exercise is that it can foster complacency. If complaint levels are measured on a branch by branch or department by department level, for example, and a target set based on best practice within the organisation, what then becomes an acceptable standard may prove below average in comparison with other organisations. While the organisation is busy measuring internally, competitors may well be gaining market share.

This is not to deny the benefits of benchmarking internally. There are 'pockets of excellence' in every organisation and identifying best practice within an organisation is a useful means of bringing about incremental change.

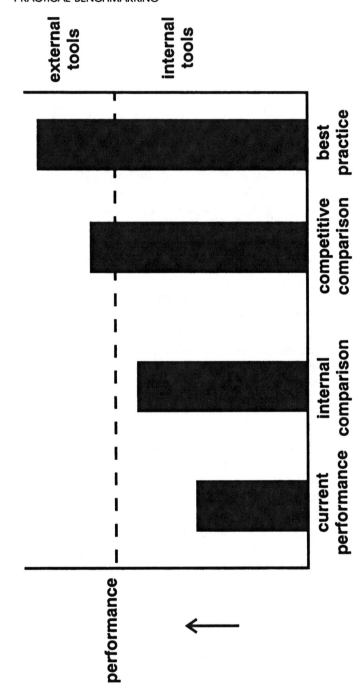

Figure 5.6 *Levels of performance improvements through benchmarking*

Soon after the formation of the healthcare company SmithKline Beecham in the early 1990s the organisation embarked on a change programme in order to get and stay ahead of its competitors. Senior managers recognised the need to promote a common way of working throughout the company which would harness employees' skills in problem solving and improvement. The 'Simply Better' way was developed as a focal point for change.

The 'Simply Better' programme consisted of a management education programme followed by a series of training for groups of employees in process improvement techniques. Benchmarking best practice throughout the organisation on a global basis is one of the tools that have been introduced as part of the process improvement toolbox. The company recognises that this is an important means of building on the best from across the organisation to create a set of enhanced working practices.

Incremental or step change

There are two types of change processes that can take place in an organisation; incremental change and step change. Incremental change involves a gradual process of small improvements which are brought about over a length of time. Step change involves radical alterations in working practices which happen swiftly and can make a major impact on organisational performance.

Often organisations who undertake internal benchmarking find that there comes a time when it is beneficial to look outwards and take an external perspective to bring about step improvements.

External benchmarking

There are two areas where external benchmarking takes place:

■ competitors; *and*

■ similar industries.

Competitive benchmarking

Competitive benchmarking can be a useful tool to determine the best practice across an industry. It is often easy to make judgements on information obtained from competitors because usually their working practices will be comparable to your own company and the market-place will be well known. Banks and building societies, for example, often use competitive benchmarking to identify standards of customer satisfaction. They, like other industries, take part in surveys administered by an independent third party which determine how each company's service quality is perceived by customers in comparison with other competitive outlets.

It is usually difficult to acquire data directly from competitors as clearly as, unsurprisingly, they can be reluctant to share information on processes which provide them with a competitive advantage. There are also legal and ethical considerations involved in gathering information from competitors. Direct dialogue with competitors can be perceived as collusion, for example.

Third party consultancy reports are a useful source of information particularly where the data is drawn on comparable performance levels. Research agencies can also broker information on competitors based on across-industry surveys. Although these reports often identify what is being done, they do not usually outline why. Also the information contained in reports is based on historical performance. It rarely encompasses details on the current state of working practices or future plans.

Where an organisation is benchmarking directly with its competitors it is imperative to draw up a framework outlining areas/questions to be covered and detailing guidelines on how the information will be used and why, together with an agreement on the time frame for the use of the information.

In our experience information gained directly from competitors should be supplemented by qualitative data obtained from customers and suppliers. These two sources can often supply information on standards of performance and how these standards are achieved. Without these further inputs competitive benchmarking is of limited benefit in bringing about change.

A definition of good service is meeting and exceeding customer expectations. The expectation of customers is based on their experiences. These in turn relate to a multiplicity of transactions with varying organisations both on a personal and a commercial basis. A more fruitful form of benchmarking, therefore, is a similar but non-competitive area.

Similar industries

Benchmarking among industries with similar character-istics is a technique which is being used by specific disciplines to increase their business focus. Advisers of the Personnel Standards League Body, for example, have compiled a database of 1,000 UK organisations in order to benchmark personnel departments against national cri-teria for best practice. The data available includes:

■ employee relations;

■ recruitment and selection;

■ performance management; *and*

■ compensation and benefits.[4]

Saratoga, the US benchmarking organisation which has moved to the UK, regularly conducts benchmarking surveys of similar UK businesses.

Advantages

There is a growing acknowledgement of the benefits of looking outwards to businesses with similar structures or constraints who may exhibit comparable practices. As these are not direct competitors, data is relatively easy to access as there is little threat to the benchmarking partner and confidentiality is assured.

Disadvantages

Although the results of most external benchmarking studies can generally be applicable to most benchmarking sponsors, as the data may not be directly comparable lessons learnt from other organisations may be difficult to apply. The organisations acting as benchmarking partners may come from different market sectors and may be different in terms of size and geographic distribution, for example. Likewise it is unrealistic to expect that best practice from one organisation can be applied to a different organisation with a different organisational culture. Step change is less likely as industry paradigms may inhibit creativity.

Best practice benchmarking

Recognising that companies or industries that are different can have similar core processes is a matter of mind set. Best practice benchmarking involves building on the success of other organisations who are considered 'best in class'. Partners are selected regardless of industry sector, business type or geographical location.

Research in the UK by the Benchmarking Centre Ltd in March 1993 indicates that only one in two companies currently benchmark against best practice. However, there is a trend among companies who have begun the benchmarking process to move from internal benchmarking to external benchmarking, and from external

1. What is good practice in our organisation? →

2. What is better than us from within similar organisations? →

3. What is 'best in class'?

Figure 5.7 *The progression of benchmarking*

benchmarking in similar organisations to undertaking benchmarking studies to identify 'best in class'.

The starting point for a best practice benchmarking study is to identify what is the 'best' . This means creating a clear definition of what is understood to be the 'best' by your company or organisation and what is recognised as such both within the organisation and externally (Figure 5.7).

Companies who have received the prestigious Malcolm Baldridge Award in the United States for example, or the Quality Award in Europe, may be considered 'best in class' in certain areas. However, your customers or employees may have different perceptions of 'the best'.

Advantages

Best practice or generic benchmarking potentially brings the highest return in terms of improvements within an organisation as it creates an external focus away from a company's own industry and as such helps in removing blinkers.

Businesses which undertake best practice benchmarking report that it is often easy to obtain data as 'best in class' organisations are often willing to share their learning experiences.

Royal Mail undertook a systematic evaluation of Baldridge Award winning companies in the United States to identify the outstanding leadership qualities needed to run a customer-focused organisation. As a result a new leadership charter has been developed for the business. Feedback on manager leadership style is provided via an upward appraisal system adapted from a benchmarking partnership with W H Smith and Avis.[5]

Disadvantages

Best practice benchmarking is potentially the most difficult. Unlike competitive benchmarking, which provides milestones against which to target improvement, setting standards to match or exceed the best involves a higher degree of change. It also involves 'thinking out of the box' - discarding the mind sets and paradigms of an organisation to adopt new ways of working.

Also, in comparison to competitive and external benchmarking programmes conducted in similar industries, best practice benchmarking normally takes longer. The difficulty comes in integrating the findings back into the sponsor organisation, particularly if the transferability of data is questioned.

Another disadvantage of the best practice route is when benchmarking becomes a one-off activity. Best practice benchmarking needs to be undertaken on a continuous basis as 'best in class' is a constantly moving target. Nevertheless, organisations which have adopted this route have been able to bring about substantial change.

When in the UK Grand Metropolitan's Smirnoff Vodka brand wished to learn from organisations which had developed global brands, it distinguished between companies which had big international brands but which dominated only a small percentage of marketplaces, and those companies which were the 'best in class' companies and had a truly global brand offering. This careful selection of best in class helped Smirnoff refocus its brand strategy.[6]

The American telephone company, Pacific Bell, used a

benchmark study to establish their call centres as 'the best of the best'. The company compiled key criteria which customers felt contributed towards an effective call handling system. A matrix was compiled and partner benchmarking companies were scored against the key criteria.

The study made Pacific Bell aware of the most important changes it needed to make in the way it organised and structured its call handling centres. Resultant changes mean that improvements have been made to credit management system, systems applications as well as personnel compensation and rewards.

Rank Xerox used the best practice principle to model their processes on the 'best in class' organisations which they identified as part of their benchmarking studies.

Customer procedures at Rank Xerox are based on those used by American Express, their research and development techniques on AT&T, and employee suggestions schemes on carpet manufacture Milliken.[7]

Consortium studies

Consortium studies, where companies interested in the same process join together to benchmark themselves, are popular with benchmarking target companies who have been identified as being 'best in class'. Instead of having to deal with ten companies who wish to benchmark the same process, they can deal with only one group representative. In addition, the sponsor participants not only share the cost in time and money but also learn a tremendous amount from each other.

Olympic athletes v tennis pros

It is not always, however, necessary to benchmark the 'best in class' to gain useful lessons. Companies who are identified as having best practices are often overwhelmed with requests.

Using smaller organisations as benchmarking partners can prove equally as fruitful. Pacific Bell, the American telephone company, undertook a survey with benchmarking partners, not considered 'best in class'. It benchmarked measures of customer satisfaction and in this way was able to save US$9million. As their benchmarking manager explained, 'You can learn from an Olympic athlete. But you can also learn from the local tennis pro.'

Learning as a benchmarking partner

ICL is an example of an organisation which has used a combination of benchmarking techniques to create competitive advantage.

ICL is involved in benchmarking in three main areas:

■ Organisations that use ICL as a benchmark;

■ Benchmarks that are initiated by task groups within ICL; *and*

■ Benchmarks which are driven by consultancy groups.

ICL recognises the benefits of being identified as a target for benchmarking. Information gained, for example, through a benchmarking study regarding the process of producing personnel computers provided ICL with feedback on customer perceptions.

In-house initiated benchmarks have increased over the last two years. This has been brought about by an increased understanding of the subject, its position and, above all, the need to improve ICL's business competitiveness.

Some benchmarks have been revisited either to widen their scope (such as investment management) or to narrow their scope (such as integration information availability). This is not to imply that the original benchmarking project was not valid but more to recognise the importance of the process to the business and the potential for further improvement that benchmarking can bring. Results have shown that ICL is well positioned against best practice.

A particularly large benchmark study has been undertaken against the processes which form part of ICL's overall customer care activity. Several processes, encompassing survey formulation and measurement criteria, have been benchmarked both internally and externally. The resulting information has been instrumental in not only enhancing the processes themselves but also providing new ideas for the overall customer care activity.

Benchmarking with the help of consultancy companies exposed both its advantages and disadvantages to ICL. Generally, the benchmark can command a wider range of resources and topic knowledge and can achieve economies of scale when it is undertaken with like-minded groups of companies. However, against this ICL found that one has to accept the compromises of the group to the processes to be benchmarked.

ICL has been involved in several benchmarks over the last two years using consultancies, notably systems architecture formulation, supply chain management and electronic systems assembly. In 1993 ICL was the main sponsor of a logistics benchmark and joint sponsor for benchmarking of project management process.*

Selecting the best partner

Finding the best partner requires extensive research. The starting point is to ask your suppliers and customers who they consider to be 'best in class'. Once you begin networking within an industry it is not surprising to find that all organisations have 'pockets of excellence'.

A key question therefore is to decide 'To whom is the process we wish to benchmark key for survival?'. A possible starting point for selecting partners is to hold a

*Reproduced by kind permission of David Smith, Operations Manager, ICL.

Benchmarking partners

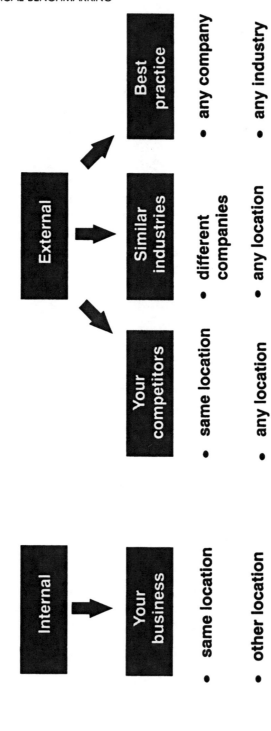

Figure 5.8 *Benchmarking partners*

meeting with project team members and to brainstorm a list of potential partners. Where possible it is useful to hold a similar exercise with customers and suppliers. The 'FT Top 500 Companies' list is also a useful source of information for selecting possible partners in the UK.

The project team also needs to consider possible selection criteria such as benchmarking partner location – national or international, language constraints and culture.

The essence of the selection criteria is to identify 'partners' – organisations which will co-operate in full agreement with the sponsor organisation in the exchange of information. In return the benchmarking sponsor must be willing to collaborate fully in the exchange of information with partners during a benchmarking exercise.

Benchmarking fast-track

A fast-track to getting started on the benchmarking route is to join a clearing house or common interest group. These organisations can help to identify potential benchmarking partners and are a useful source of information. Most benchmarking clubs provide information and can contact and screen potential collaborative businesses on the sponsors' behalf. They also normally hold a best practice database, provide publications on the topic and host regular member meetings where information can be exchanged and learning experiences shared. Further sources of information are listed in the back of this book.

Verify your choice

Once you have chosen the partner benchmarking company it is important to verify your choice through up to date background information so that you gain a better understanding of the culture and climate of the partner company.

The Benchmarking Centre Ltd undertook a survey of customer needs in the UK in March 1993. This identified that 7 out of 10 companies already practice some form of benchmarking. Of these, 95 per cent are willing to share information with the centre, and 89 per cent rate finding competent benchmarking partners as their most important requirement.

It is sometimes the case that the selection of potential partners has to be revised once further information has been obtained. Therefore, the project team will find it helpful to draw up a short-list of benchmarking candidates. They should be prepared to supplement or substitute these as the knowledge of the project team increases.

SUMMARY

■ Benchmarking is most effective when organisations reach agreement on which is the most appropriate process to benchmark.

■ There are a number of techniques for selecting key processes. These include the AHA, importance/urgency matrix and problem checklists.

■ There are four types of benchmarking partners – internal partners, external partners, be it competitive organisations or similar industries, and best practice benchmarking partners.

■ Internal benchmarking is often easiest to conduct. Competitive benchmarking is fraught with legal and ethical problems. Best practice benchmarking potentially offers the largest opportunities for improvements.

■ Benchmarking clearing houses and common interest groups provide a useful source of information for potential partners.

Checklist

Use this checklist to help you plan how to put the key points from the chapter to use within your organisation.

1. Clarify what you wish to gain from a benchmarking study. Identify the key criteria for selection of a process to benchmark within your organisation – use the techniques outlined in this chapter to make a selection.

2. Outline and discuss the advantages and disadvantages of internal benchmarking within your organisation.

3. Consider the legal and ethical considerations of competitive benchmarking in your industry sector.

4. Identify three possible benchmarking partners within an industry sector similar to your own.

5. Brainstorm which companies you consider to be 'best in class' for the process you are to review.

6. Define three best practice benchmarking partners.

7. Consider joining a benchmarking clearing house network or common interest group.

REFERENCES

1. Syrett, M (Winter 1993-4) 'The Best of Everything', *Human Resources*, Issue No. 12, page 83.
2. For more information on Analytical Hierarchy Process (AHP) see Thomas Saaty's book: *Multicriteria Decision Making* (1991) RWS Publications, US. See also: Watson, G, *Continuous Journey*, Volume 1, Number 4.
3. Carrington, L (14th June 1994) 'Measure for Measure', *Personnel Today*, pages 37-8.
4. Carrington, L (14th June 1994) 'Measure for Measure', *Personnel Today*, pages 37-8.

5. Syrett, M (Winter 1993–4) 'The Best of Everything', *Human Resources*, Issue No. 12, pages 83–4.
6. Syrett, M (Winter 1993–4) 'The Best of Everything', *Human Resources*, Issue No. 12, pages 83–4.
7. Syrett, M (Winter 1993–4) 'The Best of Everything', *Human Resources*, Issue No. 12, pages 83–4.

6

Step 3: Collect the data

The key to success in benchmarking is to collect the right information. This should be collected both quantifiably and qualitatively. If the benchmark project team focuses on only one source of information such as industry publications, it may miss important points to be gained from benchmarking partners. Likewise, if the study relies only on information gained from benchmarking partners, it may miss important details from sources such as consultants, journalists or academics.

'You need to be extremely careful in analysing what information you want' says Sheila Hughes, Head of Quality and Employee Strategy at Royal Mail. 'As with market research, asking the right questions is crucial to getting the right answers. Otherwise the whole exercise will amount to little more than industrial tourism and a colossal waste of time.'[1]

A commonly told tale is of a fact-finding benchmarking trip which took place in Japan. Members of British companies undertook a study of Japanese best practice to identify its competitive edge. The British delegation was surprised at the amount of information they were able to gather. Finally, at the end of the visit they asked one Japanese manager why the organisations they had visited had been so helpful. The manager explained that they did not mind divulging the data. In their perception the

British were asking the wrong questions – they were concentrating on past performance instead of investigating the Japanese companies' future plans. The Japanese did not mind giving the information away because they realised that by the time the British reached their current standards, they themselves would have exceeded these and continue to be ahead.

NEEDS AND CONSTRAINTS

The first task of the project team in collecting data is to identify exactly what information it needs to gather and what are its constraints. Having selected a process and thoroughly understanding its operation, the project team should have identified the following items on the checklist for data collection:

1. **Objective**.

   The project team should define the objective of the data collection stage.

2. **What does the team need to know, what would it be nice to know**?

   Encourage the team to brainstorm the essential requirements from the data collection phase.

   Point out that there is a difference between information which is essential to the project and that which is 'nice to know'.

3. **Establish quantifiable performance measures**.

   In order to make comparisons between partners and sponsor organisations it is imperative to establish what measures of performance will be used.

   Figure 6.1 shows an example of quantitative benchmarking measures which were used in a study of human resource management among ten partner companies.

Company	A	B	C
Number of employees			
Human resource staff as a percentage of total employees			
Trainers as a percentage of total employees			
Days training per head			
Training spent per head			
Absent as a percentage of time			
Leavers/years			
Dismissals/years			
Discipline/years			
Tribunals/years			

Figure 6.1 *Benchmarking measures for a human resource benchmarking study*

Here is another example of the measures which were used in a benchmarking study of marketing and sales strategy amongst competitive businesses.

■ Marketing costs per sales revenue.

■ Advertising costs per sales revenue.

■ Distribution costs.

■ Sales administration costs.

■ New products introduced.

4. **Agree what qualitative or soft measures will be used, for example company culture/communication/management style.**

5. **Decide how much information is needed, eg the number of potential partner organisations and the depth of information.**

6. **Find out what resources are available in terms of time/people/money.**

Many benchmarking studies concentrate on 'hard' performance measures and forget that often performance can only be achieved through getting the softer intangible measures correct within an organisation (Figure 6.2).

When BP Chemicals adopted a benchmarking approach to identify and aim for 'best in class' it used both hard and soft measures as a means of comparing standards. The key performance indicators it investigated included reliability, manpower and safety. It also used absolute costs obtained from consultants' databases.

However, in practice BP Chemicals found that soft data

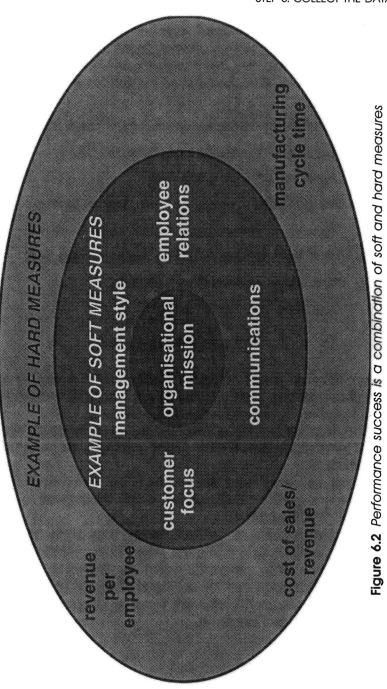

EXAMPLE OF HARD MEASURES

EXAMPLE OF SOFT MEASURES

management style

employee relations

organisational mission

customer focus

communications

revenue per employee

cost of sales/ revenue

manufacturing cycle time

Figure 6.2 *Performance success is a combination of soft and hard measures*

was a better means of comparison. The working practices of the partner, size of organisation, organisational culture, employee attitude all proved useful benchmarks. The checklist of comparisons they used included:

- *Activity* – operations, maintenance function.

- *Function* – IT, distribution, finance, HR.

- *Organisation* – core, support.

- *Relationships* – reporting lines, teams, layers.

- *Hierarchy* – managers, professionals, workers.

- *Working practices* – shift systems, outsourcing.

- *Technology* – competitiveness, use.

SOURCES OF INFORMATION

There are four major sources of information available to benchmarking project teams. These are desk research, third parties, direct exchange and site visits.

The first two sources of information, desk research and third parties, do not involve direct contact with potential partners.

Direct exchange and site visits allow benchmarking partners to gather information with employees from partner organisations.

The temptation of project team members at the beginning of the data collection phase is to make contact immediately with potential partners. However, much useful information can be obtained from other sources and provides a useful learning exercise for project team members in familiarisation.

Desk research

Benchmarking project teams are often surprised at the amount of information they can find available without leaving the organisation. The first part of data collection can begin in-house where sources such as company libraries, corporate publications, directories, data bases and industry journals may provide useful background information.

Other sources of information external to the organisation include market research companies' reports, trade associations, industry networks, media reports, seminars and conferences, as well as suppliers and customers, professional institutions and consultants.

As there is potentially a wealth of sources available, experienced project teams draw up an action plan for undertaking this analytical phase of research. Where possible it is useful for all project team members to undertake part of this research exercise as they will all then become familiar with the background to the project and process during the course of their research. An action plan should outline what information needs to be gathered, where it can be gathered from, who will undertake each activity and when the activity will take place.

Third parties

In addition to examining internal documents and publicly available information, third parties such as consultants and research firms provide a useful source of data.

If organisations are interested in matching up to industry standards then bringing in a consultancy with the information to hand is often a fast route to gaining information. However, a disadvantage of using consultants to gather data is that it distances project team members from the process, and a lack of ownership of the information may ensue.

Benchmarking Study : Information Gathering Action Plan			
Information Requirement	Potential Sources	Responsibility	Deadline

Figure 6.3 *Information-gathering action plan*

Where consultants and research firms are particularly useful, however, is in the gathering of information about competitors.

Reviewing results of data gathering

Before contacting third parties, project team members need to be sure exactly what information they require. It is helpful, therefore, to compile a list of key measures (soft and hard) and to check off what information has been gathered by desk research. From this checklist a list of data which is still required and potentially available from third parties can be compiled.

CONTACTING POTENTIAL PARTNERS

There are two methods which can be adopted in obtaining information directly from potential partners - indirect exchange and face to face visits.

Initial contact

Before making initial contact with potential partners the project team should take time to consider if anyone in the team or their organisation already has contact with the potential partner, or knows of anyone who is familiar with the potential partner or organisation. It is easier to make contact in this way rather than to 'phone or write 'out of the blue'. Some organisations are naturally suspicious of unsolicited approaches. They may also be hesitant about the benefits of participating in a bench-marking study, particularly if this is the first approach they have received.

To contribute to effective, efficient and ethical bench-marking, individuals need to agree for themselves and their organisations to abide by the principle of bench-marking with other organisations. The underlying tenet is not to ask for information that you as the sponsor organisation would not be prepared to divulge about your own organisation.

The principles of benchmarking encompass:

■ confidentiality;

■ legality;

■ exchange;

■ use of information;

■ first party contact;

■ third party contact; *and*

■ preparation.

Team members should decide who should be the entry point of contact within the potential partner organisation. For example, at what level is the information which is required likely to be most readily available? What is the protocol within the potential partner organisation for this type of exercise? It could be, for example, that the people from the potential benchmarking partner who appear in published articles, are the most appropriate point of contact. It could be that a trade association will be able to point the team in the right direction.

A further question to discuss is who from the team should make the contact with the potential partner organisation, or indeed with partners within your own organisation.

Finally, the team needs to consider, agree and rehearse what introductions/explanations should be given to potential partner organisations regarding the purpose of the project.

When assembling information on behalf of your own company, therefore, it is helpful to explain the background to the project to those providing the information so that they fully understand why the information is required. It is particularly important to emphasise the cooperative nature of the exercise and the mutual benefits to be gained.

A typical introductory discussion/written correspondence with potential benchmarking partners would therefore outline:

- background to the project;

- a brief synopsis of the information required from the potential partner;

- explanation of what's in it for them (stressing the mutual benefits);

- estimation of timescale requirements;

- questions regarding the best method of collecting information from the potential partner; *and*

- information regarding the best people to contact for access to the data within the potential partner organisation.

Direct exchange

Benchmarking with external companies is often associated with site visits. In fact site visits are often the last port of call in a benchmarking exercise. Direct exchange of information can take place via such media as:

- telephone surveys;

- written questionnaires;

- video conferencing; *and*

- tele-conferencing.

Questionnaires

Questionnaires are a useful data collection tool to solicit information and opinion from benchmarking partners.

105

In preparing a questionnaire the team should decide what questions to ask and the ability of the benchmarking audience to answer these. The design of the questionnaire should be logical; the team will need to check that the questions are clear and unambiguous and will provide relevant responses. It is useful to pilot the questionnaire in your own organisation before preparing a final document. A typical design will include:

■ introduction, detailing objectives of your benchmarking study and details of the sponsor company;

■ outline of measures of performance to be used;

■ actual performance of partner organisation; *and*

■ description of business practices to achieve this performance.

Interviews

Gathering information by the interview process provides the project team with a useful insight into the process. When BP Chemicals decided to benchmark its HR practices the starting point was to understand its own process better by interviewing a cross-section of employees across the company.

Interviews can take place with benchmarking partners on a direct or indirect basis. Like written questionnaires, they provide a quantitative measure of performance. They are the fastest way to get basic details of the process and to begin to understand the intangible aspects of the partner organisation.

Like written questionnaires, in preparation for the interview the interviewer needs to identify the issues and questions to be discussed and prepare an agenda. The project team member who is conducting the interview needs to listen carefully to answers and record these as clearly as possible. He or she will need to clarify vague responses and ensure that all replies are noted and the results of the interview documented.

Site visits

Site visits are not necessary to every benchmarking study. However, they do provide project team members with a useful insight into how the process is conducted which will supplement the information from other sources on what the process in the partner organisation achieves.

The fear of many potential benchmarking partners is that site visits can be a time consuming and haphazard experience. Careful planning and preparation can overcome potential partners' initial fears. Prior to the visit project team members should establish how feasible it is to see the process in action at the partner organisation, which part of the organisation is most appropriate to visit, who should be involved both from the project team and the partner organisation in the visit, when is the best time to visit and how long the visit should last.

In preparing for the visit it is beneficial to meet with the partner organisation to explain the purpose of the visit on a face to face basis and to ensure that all aspects are arranged prior to the visit.

There are a number of protocols or 'visiting rules' which apply to site visits:

- Always agree a formal agenda with careful timing before each visit.

- Discuss and agree your host's expectation of the visit and their requirements as well as your own.

- Offer and be prepared to sign a confidentiality agreement with the host organisation.

- Prepare and use a questionnaire or interview checklist as a basis for discussion.

- If at all possible, see the process in action and speak to the people involved.

- Be open and honest in exchanges with the partner organisation and ensure that information flows both ways.

- Record information about the process while it is fresh in your mind.

- Make notes during the visit.

Look, listen, question

Experience shows that site visits are best undertaken by more than one project team member. In this way the outcome will be a variety of impressions and information as each person reacts in a different way to the visit.

Using your eyes is important - impressions are a valuable means of identifying 'the way things are done around here'.

Listening is also an important aspect of a site visit. Listen to people around you, try to identify soft issues such as culture/management style, communication levels.

Constantly ask questions - how does the process work, why does it work this way, what makes the host company different from its competitors? Are the performance measures it uses similar to your own?

The 'why, why, why' technique is helpful here. The project team members ask the question 'Why is the process undertaken in this way?' A reply is given, for example, 'Because our customers need delivery within three days'. The project team member then asks, 'Why do they need delivery within three days?' The response could be 'Because the reps have told them this'. The project team members should then ask 'Why?'. And so on, until a full understanding is achieved of the process and the reasons for it.

Validate the data

Use the site visit to check the data you have already

collected from other sources on the partner organisation. If there are discrepancies, ask for clarification. Seek further information on performance indicators as required.

Recording the visit

Following the visit you will need to document the outcome within one or two days while the information is to hand. Send a copy of the report to the host company so that they can check the validity of the data and the conclusions. Remember to include your own comparative company information in the report so that the benchmarking partner benefits from your visit.

Shortly after the visit and the report has been compiled the project team members who have gone to the site should verbally present back to the other team members their findings. This gives the team an opportunity to share both the hard data that has been acquired and also to gain an impression of some of the softer, cultural issues. Where possible both the report and the verbal debrief should contain practical examples.

Texas Instruments uses taping of best practices to show how work is accomplished at their different sites. A benchmarking study at half a dozen sites across the US and Asia shows differences in inventory turns of the order of five to thirty. Documenting and recording how the process was accomplished helped sub-standard sites to identify the gaps in their performance.

Return visits

You may be asked by the benchmarking partner to host a return visit so that the partner company can see how processes work at your site. This provides a helpful insight into what the benchmarking partner believes you are getting right within your organisation and their perception of your own areas for improvement.

Documentation

Although a benchmarking study does not need to be bureaucratic, a small amount of documentation is needed to capture learning points and information gained from benchmarking partners. Recording data also allows the project team to identify what further information is required and to follow this up with other organisations at a later date.

Also, unless information is documented time can be wasted in re-collating key measures when further benchmarking site visits take place.

SUMMARY

■ The quality of data which is collected from benchmarking partners is only as good as the quality of the questions asked. Before beginning a benchmarking data collection phase, project team members should determine their exact requirements and constraints.

■ Sources of information on benchmarking partners include desk research, third party information, direct exchange and site visits.

■ Desk research is an essential part of all benchmarking activity. Third party sources are useful as a gateway to competitor information. The most frequently used source of information is direct exchange. Site visits are not always necessary and when they take place require careful planning. Time should be taken in the preparation of questionnaires and interview checklist to be used with benchmarking partners.

■ There is a protocol for site visits to ensure that a full understanding of the process is acquired and how this is achieved.

■ Documentation of site visits and data collated is an important aspect of the benchmarking programme.

CHECKLIST

Use this checklist to help you plan how to put the key points from the chapter to use within your organisation.

1. Prepare a list of questions to be asked of benchmarking partners.

2. Identify both soft and hard issues which need to be discovered.

3. Prepare an action plan outlining sources of information, who will collect the information, where and when.

4. Compile a questionnaire and interview checklist for data collection.

REFERENCES

1. Syrett, M (Winter 1993–4) 'The Best of Everything', *Human Resources*, Issue No. 12, pages 83–4.

7

Step 4: Analyse data and identify gaps

Once data has been collected the task of the project team is to interpret the information they have acquired and identify areas for improvement. This analysis takes two forms:

■ review of the data; *and*

■ preparation of gap analysis.

REVIEW ANALYSIS OF DATA

The first step is to quantify the differences in the information gained from benchmarking partners. Draw up a matrix grid itemising the performance indicators in the left hand column and list the various benchmarking partners along the top horizontal column. Then enter the data that you have captured in the appropriate column (Figure 7.1).

Quantitative differences should be relatively straightforward to calculate. It is possible to identify performance means as well as calculating differences between one benchmarking partner and another.

Turk Enustan, Director of Corporate Benchmarking for Eastman Kodak, cites an example for one of its manufacturing divisions which began gathering benchmarking

Performance indicator	Site A	Site B	Site C	Site D
Revenue per employee	£5,975	£23,110	£29,000	£37,000
Cost of sales/marketing	10%	3%	5.5%	8%

Figure 7.1 *Example of data analysis*

data internally. It compared six different products made at seven sites around the world. Big differences in quality, cost and inventory levels were discovered. This made the company recognise the potential savings to be made by matching each operating unit to the best in each category.

There are various tools which can be used during data analysis. Chapter 4 outlined the use of process flow charts and fishbone diagrams as a means of understanding an organisation's processes. These techniques can equally be used with external or internal benchmarking partners to understand better how they operate.

There are also a number of other techniques which can be used to gather detailed information, such as bar charts, histograms, pie charts and scattergrams.

Scattergrams, for example, can be used to study the possible relationship between one variable and another and to test for possible cause and effect relationships.

A bar chart is a helpful starting point for identifying the most important elements in a process through the use of different measurement scales.

These techniques are well known as analysis tools and are often used as part of a TQM programme. They allow information to be analysed and displayed graphically.

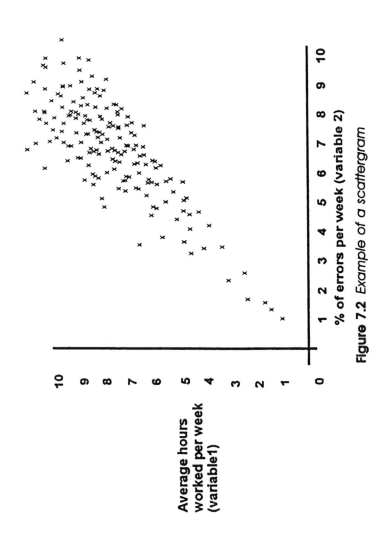

Figure 7.2 Example of a scattergram

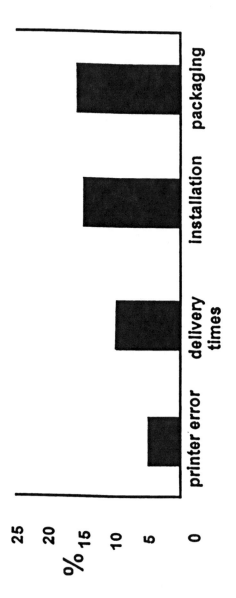

Figure 7.3 *Example of a bar chart*

Soft measures

Although a review of hard data provides an easy means of measurable comparisons, what it does not identify is how the performance measures are achieved. The 'soft issues' surrounding each benchmarking partner need to be considered and analysed in a similar format to hard quantifiable data.

As indicated earlier it is often the soft issues which provide more information to project team members on why a process is successful. Project team members may return, for example, from a site visit having identified that the partner organisation has an open management style, that its employees seem highly motivated and it has high levels of customer satisfaction. These perceptions need to be quantified if analysis is to be made on a comparative basis. What is meant, for example, by high levels of motivation or open management style?

Within each organisation there will be performance measures which can be applied to the soft issues. Motivation, for example, can be measured in terms of employee absenteeism or sickness or the number of suggestions made to a suggestion scheme. Open management style can be measured in terms of the number of layers in a structure of an organisation, how often managers gather and act on feedback, the number of communication vehicles within an organisation and policies relating to empowerment and devolvement of responsibilities. Customer satisfaction can be measured, for example, in terms of the lifetime value of a customer, customer retention, number of repeat orders and number and type of complaints. Figure 7.4 gives an example of an analysis of both hard and soft measures.

UNDERSTANDING THE ORGANISATIONAL ENVIRONMENT

In order for direct comparison to be made between

117

Competitive benchmarking analysis for call out service comparing competitors A, B and C

Customer requirement	Performance measurement	A	B	C
Price	Based on 3 hour call out	£35	£29	£50
Delivery	Average time for engineer to arrive	3 hrs	2.5 hrs	4.5 hrs
Customer service score	Customer satisfaction with service	90%	100%	70%

Figure 7.4 A benchmarking matrix for a call-out service

different benchmarking partners, project team members need to understand the different environments in which the partner organisations operate.

There are a number of tools which can be used to generate an understanding of the organisational context for each benchmarking partner.

Forcefield analysis

This is a technique which encourages the user to identify driving forces in an organisation. On one side of a sheet of paper are written the forces which encourage effective processes. On the opposite side project team members need to identify the forces inhibiting the effective management of processes within an organisation (Figure 7.5).

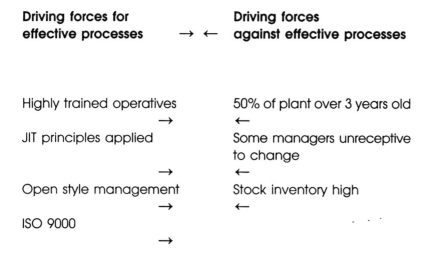

Driving forces for effective processes → ← **Driving forces against effective processes**

Highly trained operatives	50% of plant over 3 years old
→	←
JIT principles applied	Some managers unreceptive to change
→	←
Open style management	Stock inventory high
→	←
ISO 9000	
→	

Figure 7.5 *A force field analysis for a manufacturing company*

Five forces analysis

Michael Porter has devised a useful framework for determining an organisation's competitive position. This analysis can help the team explain differences in performance across varying industry sectors. This tool is particularly useful in comparing best practices as it provides a framework for developing measured criteria.

Professor Porter's concept is that competitive advantage is a result of the size and structure of the industry in which an organisation operates, the competitive environment and the bargaining power of customers and suppliers.

In making comparisons across industries a matrix can be developed using each of the five forces to help identify similar and dissimilar competitive environments based on Porter's concept.

Much information will be gathered as part of a benchmarking study which may not be truly relevant to the exercise. A tip here is to use a matrix format to distil information. This encourages project team members to identify the critical factors in performance and therefore to make direct comparison.

GAP ANALYSIS

Identifying gaps in performance

Successful data analysis should result in a comparison being able to be made between different performance criteria and best practice methods. Once the analysis has been completed, therefore, the next step is to identify your own company's performance measures and to make comparison with other benchmarking partners. In this way target levels of performance can be discussed and agreed and a further comparison made between target performance and actual performance.

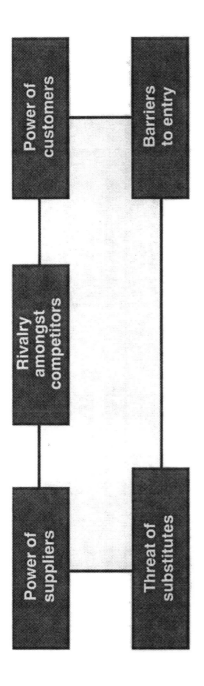

Figure 7.6 *Porter's five forces*

Actual performance	Target performance	Best practice method	Current method
Price : £35	£30	Price quoted at time of call. Details of service provided.	Price given to customer after job completed.
Delivery : 3 hours	2 hours	Service engineers use mobile phones and call in for next job.	Service engineers report back to base after each job.
Customer service : Score : 90%	Score : 100% Faster delivery	Call time agreed with customer on booking. Customer called back after job completed to confirm quality and satisfaction.	No call time given to customer. No follow up quality check.

Figure 7.7 *Actual versus target performance matrix*

Where the internal standard is higher than the target performance this is termed a 'positive' gap. Where the performance levels in place in an organisation are lower than the target performance or best practice this is called a 'negative' gap.

The task of the project team is to quantify the size of the gap in actual versus target or best practice performance. As well as quantifying this it is important to state the causes for differences in performance – what is best practice versus the current in-house practices.

Figure 7.7 is an example of a matrix outlining actual versus target performance, identifying best practice methods and providing a synopsis of current methods in-house. This provides an easy to digest summary of the gaps in performance.

In the early stages of benchmarking it is probable that most gap analysis will be negative. The exception to this may be where in conducting a benchmarking study organisations find there are 'pockets of excellence' within their organisation. The skill here is to build on what is good within the host organisation and to take on board improvements which can be identified in benchmarking partners.

At this stage a decision needs to be made:

■ Should the organisation seek to match or better the best practice?

■ Has the organisation the capability to achieve the desired improvement? What is now best practice among benchmarking partners will undoubtedly change over time, so the organisation needs to decide at what level to target improvements – at existing best practices or beyond. If best practices far exceed current organisational performance it may be more realistic to set incremental targets for improvements which can be made on a gradual basis rather than instigating step change (Figure 7.8).

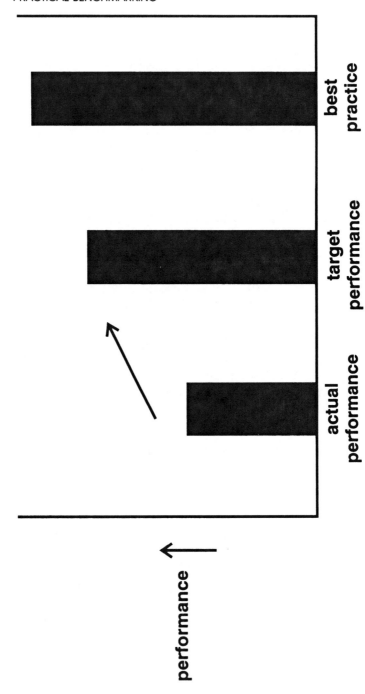

Figure 7.8 *Example of targeted incremental change*

Chapter 8 outlines an approach to planning improvements and how these can be put in to action.

SUMMARY

- This chapter outlines techniques for analysing data and identifying gaps in performance.

- Once data has been collected, it needs to be analysed and reviewed so that a comparison can be made between the performance of benchmarking partners and the sponsor organisation.

- In addition to making comparisons with 'hard' data, organisations should look at 'soft' issues and attempt to quantify these.

- There are a number of techniques available for analysing data. It is helpful to construct a matrix to make comparisons.

- Once the information has been collected a gap analysis can be prepared, outlining target performance versus actual performance.

- At this stage a decision needs to be made whether to aim for incremental or step change.

CHECKLIST

Use this checklist to help you plan how to put the key points from the chapter to use within your organisation.

1. Draw up a matrix of performance indicators from your benchmarking partners in order to make a comparison with your own organisation.

2. Where possibly quantify your qualitative perceptions.

3. Use some of the techniques outlined in this chapter such as scattergrams, and five forces analysis as interpretive tools.

4. Produce a gap analysis to identify differences and targets for improvement.

5. Decide whether your organisation should aim for step or incremental change.

8

Step 5: Plan and action improvements

Having identified both the size of gap in performance and potential causes, the next step is to identify and prioritise areas of change and to draw up a plan for improvements.

Often benchmark studies identify a number of improvements that can be made. It is important to attach priorities to these so that efforts are worthwhile. There are various methods of identifying which changes need to be addressed.

All Johnson & Johnson Medical Corporation employees in the US are introduced to benchmarking as one of the components of their 'quality journey' training.

The emphasis of benchmarking studies is to identify improvement opportunities. Project team members are each asked to make a list of ten things they learned from benchmarking. From this list the organisation prefers to implement one strong change, rather than trying to accomplish all ten items.

Prioritisation

As Figure 8.1 illustrates, although it is useful to quantify the gap in performance it is also imperative to refer back to the decision-making criteria which are used for identifying each process to analyse.

Performance Indicator	Actual performance	Target performance	Gap	Customer priority
Speed of check in	7	8	<1>	1
Baggage handling	5	7	<2>	2
On time departures	6	8	<2>	3

Figure 8.1 A performance matrix showing customer priorities

In this case this is customer priorities. In this example a customer satisfaction survey was completed in which customers were asked to rank their priorities in terms of the service elements the company provided. The research survey demonstrated that speed of checking was the first priority followed by baggage handling. A third priority was on-time departures. Therefore in the example, although the performance gaps for baggage handling and on-time departures are larger than for speed of checking, as the latter is the first priority for customers it should be addressed by the organisation first.

Likewise, when the project team decides which of the two other service performance indicators need improvement next, they will find that the customer satisfaction survey indicates that baggage handling is more important to customers than on-time departures. Therefore, although the organisation needs to tackle all three areas, the matrix provides insight into the order for improvements.

Cost/benefit analysis

A further method of deciding changes to be made is to undertake a cost/benefit analysis. This outlines the potential cost to the organisation of suggested improvements. This normally encompasses the areas of financial outlay, time, people and other tangible and intangible resources. At the same time the benefits to the organisation can be quantified, such as customer retention, increased levels of customer satisfaction, lower levels of down time and increased work in progress.

Significant improvement matrix

A consideration the project team should make in putting forward suggestions for improvement is the level of upheaval the improvement will involve to the organisation

129

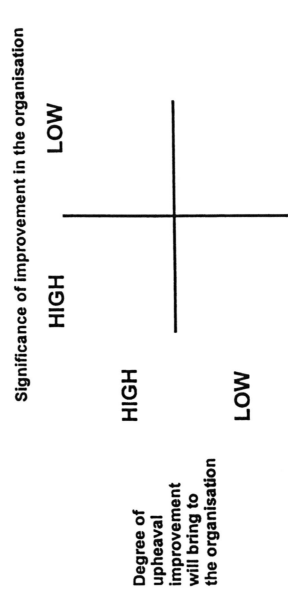

Figure 8.2 *Significant improvement matrix*

in comparison with the significant change it will bring towards meeting corporate objectives. A simple matrix outlining importance and upheaval can be constructed as a basis for discussion (Figure 8.2).

This is not to say that change which is significant and which brings upheaval should not be tackled. However, a decision should be made whether to address a number of incremental improvements or to aim for step change. This decision will be easier to make once all the improvement options have been considered.

THE CHANGE OPTIONS

There are a number of tools available to plan for improvement in the process which has been benchmarked.

Brainstorming

Brainstorming is a useful technique to identify potential changes. It is the quantity not quality of ideas that are important during a brainstorming session.

The session should be led by the project team leader, whose task is to record every idea, no matter how frivolous or irrelevant it may seem. Using a flip chart provides a focal point for this process. One idea should generate others; when ideas run out the team can develop variations on those already generated.

It is not advisable to evaluate ideas during a 'live' session. Team members should review the list at other subsequent meetings and then evaluate each idea.

Scenario development

An alternative means of brainstorming is to develop scenarios for possible future versions of the current

131

process. This takes the traditional format of brainstorming a stage further in that, rather than only trying to generate a list of ideas, ideas are linked to scenarios. The implications of each scenario can then be evaluated at a further session.

For example, alternative scenarios for improving the process in a manufacturing company may be:

1. To outsource part of the manufacturing processes in line with other best practices.

2. To increase the number of machines per line, in line with competitor industries.

3. To increase staff training and devolve responsibility in line with best practice.

Once a scenario has been developed for each alternative, the pros and cons can be identified for each option.

Greenfield design

When the carrier company TNT undertakes a benchmarking exercise it has no pre-conceived ideas on how the improved process should be designed. The benchmarking project team asks 'What does the customer want, what is the best that can be done?', in order to bring about improvements.

To develop creative new processes or ideas it is often useful to 'think out of the box'. This means designing a process without being restricted by current practices and problems. The project team would therefore develop a process from the beginning as if no process were currently in place. The term 'greenfield design' originates from the building of a new facility on an open, undeveloped piece of land, rather than trying to improve an existing building.

A starting point is to ask what would the customer do if the customer were designing the process for us? What is the minimum that must be done?

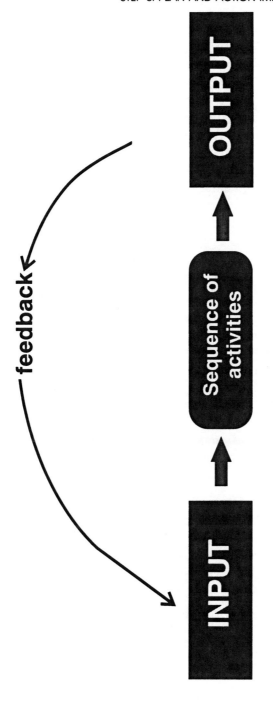

Figure 8.3 *The stages of a process*

The team starts with a blank sheet of paper and determines the critical features of the process. These can be classified into inputs, activities and outputs which lead to a result. Normally, a process needs a feedback loop such as customer satisfaction and retention to ensure the effectiveness of the process.

The team document their thoughts and formulate a process following the ideal flow, keeping the process as simple as possible. It is at this stage that comparison can be made with existing processes and areas for change identified (Figure 8.4).

Re-designed process flow

If it is not possible, due to organisational constraints, to develop a process from scratch, an alternative method of re-designing a process is to compare the activities it encompasses with the best practices that the project team has identified among benchmarking partners. In this way redundant steps can be spotlighted and critical features of the process highlighted. Again the flow should be kept as simple as possible and the critical steps in the suggested improved process documented (Figure 8.5).

Setting targets

The project team should at this stage have identified areas for improvement. It is at this point that specific recommendations need to be made on the targets to aim for in the future.

TNT's benchmarking team developed a checklist for setting targets, which should:

■ stretch the capabilities;

■ be specific;

■ be concrete;

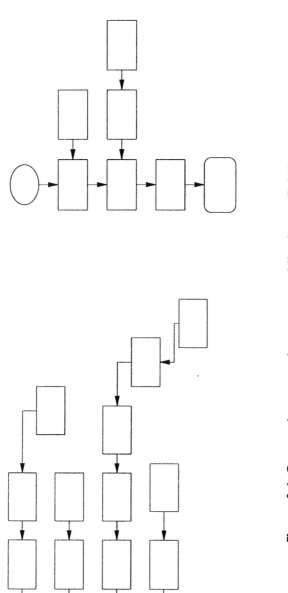

Figure 8.4 Comparing current process and the 'greenfield' process

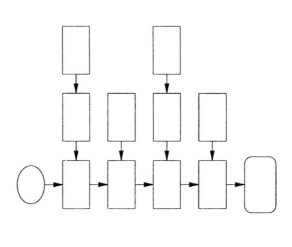

Best practice process

The current process

136

Figure 8.5 *Re-designing the process*

■ be measurable;

■ have a time commitment established;

■ have accountability clearly defined; *and*

■ agree targets with parties involved.

Before setting targets the project team should check that the information they have obtained to date is accurate and comprehensive.

PREPARING RECOMMENDATIONS

It is probable that the targets the team sets for improvement will have to be agreed by other people throughout the organisation. When preparing recommendations it is helpful to consider who needs to agree the targets and what their decision criteria will be. For example, if a project team is reporting back to the senior management group what likely questions may they pose? How do the targets for improvement meet the organisation's existing mission or vision? The team also needs to consider the resources necessary to complete the project successfully. Is there the ability in house to undertake the changes? If not, how can the resources be found? What are the implications and the cost involved?

Preparing an action plan

In putting forward recommendations for improvement the team needs to document fully what the improvements involve, how the changes will be implemented, and when. The team also needs to outline who will take responsibility for implementation. In developing a plan for improvement the benefits of the proposed improvement should be quantified, for example:

■ increase market share;

- higher client satisfaction;

- higher customer satisfaction;

- increased productivity; *and*

- less re-work.

Often, the improvement may lead to a longer term solution, yet to reach this solution involves a number of shorter term activities. These should be broken down to show each stage of the implementation plan.

Where large-scale change is proposed, the organisation may decide to pilot the new process as a means of testing its success. Here measures of success for the pilot must be set. After the pilot period comparison can then be made with an existing process in a similar part of the organisation.

Set a timescale for the pilot and gather as much information from process users in the test area in order to evaluate its effectiveness. Should the result prove positive it is then possible to cascade the implementation of the process on a larger scale throughout the organisation, drawing on the learning from the pilot area.

Commitment

In preparing an action plan the project team should consider what commitment is needed and from whom for each part of the improvement process. Often the drivers and enablers for change are not identified before a change process takes place. The visible commitment of the project sponsor can prove invaluable. The team also needs to evaluate who else throughout the organisation at all levels will champion its cause.

Allocate responsibilities

The project team should be firm in its recommendations

of who should be responsible for each stage of the implementation plan, including a timetable for review. Where possible link improvements to individual's personal objectives to ensure that there is more likelihood of changes taking place.

Attention to detail

There are no quick fixes to bringing about improvements. Setting targets and working to a plan will facilitate change only when attention is paid to every aspect that needs to improve.

The result of questioning and challenging practices led to a number of changes in the way BP Chemicals operate, for example. Its benchmarking study identified areas where 'best in class' companies had a higher performance level than its own. For example:

■ 'Best in class' companies had a higher ratio of core to support staff. In response BP Chemicals set itself a target of decreasing the number of its support staff and incorporated some functions into manufacturing.

■ There were six layers from the top to the bottom of the organisation prior to benchmarking. In best practice organisations the number stood at four to five. Subsequently, BP Chemicals delayered and empowered their employees to match the structure in best practice companies.

■ The ratio of technicians to production staff was higher in BP Chemicals than in 'best in class' organisations. In response one BP Chemical site has introduced a 'team technician'.

■ US sites had detailed emissions inventories while UK didn't. All BP Chemical sites now measure emissions and publish emissions inventories.

■ The number of purchase orders below £500 was high

in BP Chemicals in comparison with 'best in class' companies. The organisation reduced numbers of suppliers and items.

Communicate findings

When preparing recommendations for improvements, the project team needs to consider how its findings will be communicated and understood by everyone throughout the organisation. Initially, the number of people who will have knowledge of the benchmarking process will be few. This number will probably be restricted to project team members and members of senior management. An awareness of benchmarking and its benefits needs to be spread throughout the business. General Electrics, for example, normally forms teams of ten people to under-take benchmarking studies but their findings are widely circulated and also included as part of their management development school.

When recommendations are made to senior managers they probably require an outline timetable of what should happen and when. However, change will not take place without involving other people throughout the organisa-tion. It is most likely at this stage that the project team will expand or disband and reform with additional, new members. These will include specialists and other people involved in the process who were not initially on the project team.

The results of the benchmarking study need to be communicated sympathetically and in a participative manner throughout the organisation. As benchmarking may be a new concept, the initial communication should include such information as:

- What are the principles of benchmarking?

- Why has the organisation undertaken a study?

■ How does benchmarking link with the organisation's aims and visions for the future?

■ Who was involved in the benchmarking study?

■ What took place and when?

■ What were the results of the study?

■ What will the benefits mean to individuals in the organisation?

OVERCOMING RESISTANCE TO CHANGE

Benchmarking is just one implement in an armoury of tools which can be used to bring about change within an organisation. It is often best used as part of a programme of on-going improvement. Whether the organisation is used to change or not, a typical reaction of both managers and staff who may be potentially involved in the change is 'why?'.

There may be several reasons for this resistance which often manifests itself in the 'not invented here' syndrome. 'It has nothing to do with us so why bother, we are doing OK, so why change?' The more fundamental the change the more resistance that will be encountered.

Blockages to change

A lack of commitment to change can be caused by a number of issues:

■ lack of understanding of the need to change;

■ fear of consequence of change;

■ safety of status quo;

■ desire for a quick fix rather than long-term improvement;

- lack of management focus; *and*

- lack of understanding of organisational objectives.

When any change takes place the natural human reaction is initially to deny the changes and to resist them either verbally or through behaviour (or a lack of it). Once the change begins to take place some people will be more receptive and begin to explore the possible benefits – what's in it for them and how will it affect their working practices? – before deciding whether or not to be committed to change. People go through a series of responses to change (Figure 8.6).

Communicate the need for change

Resistance to change will decrease as people become more aware of the reasons for the change. Therefore two way communication is the key to a successful improvement programme. Likewise, management must be seen to take a strong lead in the process and to be supportive of the changes.

Results of many change programmes have identified that middle managers are the most likely group to resist change as they feel sandwiched between the desires of senior management to bring about improvement and members of staff who may doubt the benefit of change for them. As many benchmarking studies will identify, it is often not *what* is done but *how* that brings about successful practices. Rover's collaboration with Honda, for example, has addressed not only the performance measures that are used, but also the management processes which bring about the standards of excellence. If the management of an organisation is not committed to lead the change process, then the project team's proposals will fall on stony ground.

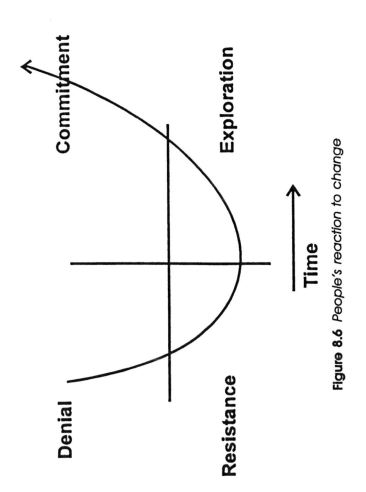

Figure 8.6 *People's reaction to change*

Leadership

One of the fundamental issues which the project team must address in developing an action plan is who will lead the process. What style of leadership is required to bring about improvement? Is this leadership style current within the organisation? If not, what needs to change?

As organisations are moving towards flatter, more customer-focused structures, the role of the manager has had to change from one of cop or police officer to coach. The traditional command style of management is no longer applicable and a more participative and facilitative approach is required (Figure 8.7). The project team should therefore consider management style as part of their overall recommendations.

Old style organisation	New style organisation
Internally focused	Focused on the customer
Many layers	Fewer layers
Manager as cop	Manager as coach
Decisions taken by few	Decisions taken by many

Figure 8.7 *Old style and new style organisation*

Language

A final tip: project team members need to formulate their recommendations and develop an implementation plan in a language which is readily understandable to everyone throughout the organisation. Too often jargon creeps into business use and what may easily be understood by the project team may not be common knowledge among

144

the rest of the business. This can distance the rest of the organisation and hinder the concept of continuous improvement.

SUMMARY

- Having identified gaps in performance, this chapter sets out methods for prioritising improvement areas.

- There are several techniques for planning improved processes including brainstorming, scenario development, greenfield design and process re-design.

- Before developing a plan for improvement, targets for change should be clearly identified. An action plan needs to be developed which outlines the steps in bringing about improvement.

- Recommendations need to be clearly communicated to both senior management and all parts of the business.

- The project team should be aware of the resistance to change and identify potential blockages.

- In addition the team should identify the management style which is needed to lead the change process, recognising that this can be a key driver in bringing about improvement.

CHECKLIST

Use this checklist to help you plan how to put the key points from the chapter to use within your organisation.

1. Adopt one of the methods indicated in the chapter for prioritising areas for improvement.

2. Use brainstorming techniques to redesign your process using the greenfield design principle.

3. Prepare a detailed action plan, identifying what should change, when and how and who will be responsible.

4. Ensure measures of success are included in the action plan.

5. Consider how you will communicate your findings and put forward recommendations.

6. Consider the role of management in bringing about change.

7. Identify potential process champions throughout the organisation and how they may be used as catalysts for change.

9

Step 6: Review

The length of time needed for the implementation phase of a benchmarking programme can vary greatly according to the complexity of the improvements that are being introduced. If implementation is lengthy, the temptation is to move on to the next project as in increasingly competitive environments the pace of change is relentless. Alternatively, the team may become involved in the detail of the implementation plan without taking the opportunity to stand back and review what has been achieved, how and why.

It would be useful to review the progress of a study at least twice, for example, during any major re-engineering programme. At the beginning of the process managers can use competitive analyses, customer information, operating performance and benchmarking to identify key processes to re-engineer. Then when re-design begins, they can benchmark 'best in class' examples to create the new design.

MONITORING PROGRESS

Benchmarking studies should be monitored on a regular basis. Project teams do not have to wait until a benchmarking study is complete. Progress checks are useful throughout the development of a benchmarking study. Two possible types of review can take place:

■ review of the results of the benchmarking project in terms of organisational performance; *and*

■ review of the results of the benchmarking process in terms of the learning which has been gained and how this has been applied.

AT&T in the US, for example, believes so strongly in the learning which has been gained from benchmarking that it offers external workshops to those who wish to attend from outside the organisation to promote the learning it has acquired from benchmarking. In 1993 AT&T Paradyne undertook 15 benchmarking studies of which 12 were completed. This involved training for 102 team members, contacting over a hundred companies and participating in two external surveys. The quickest time a benchmarking study took to complete was 35 days.

REVIEWING RESULTS

At the beginning of a benchmarking study the project team will have set overall objectives and measures of success. The key questions to be asked, therefore, when undertaking a review are:

■ Has the study met its objectives?

■ What has changed and why?

■ Have the goalposts changed? (The objectives of the project may, for example, have been altered in the light of benchmarking information received.)

■ What impact have the improvements had on the organisation? (Incremental change or step change?)

■ What have been the most significant improvements brought about by this project team?

■ What evidence is there of change in the process?

- What is the value of the changes to the organisation?
- Were the measures that have been benchmarked correct?
- Was the organisation willing to change?
- What were the barriers to change?
- How have these been overcome?

It is useful to gather information via an internal audit using interviews or questionnaires in response to these questions so that a formal review can take place. In preparation for the review, project team members may find it useful to prepare a SWOT analysis:

- What *strength* has emerged as a result of the process?
- What *weaknesses* has the study thrown up?
- What *opportunities* are there for further development?
- What are the *threats* to further development?

It is useful to summarise the findings of the SWOT analysis in note form on one sheet of paper.

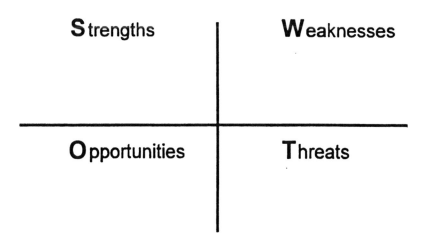

Figure 9.1 *SWOT analysis*

Once a SWOT has been compiled, project team members should identify:

■ how they can build on their strengths;

■ how to overcome weaknesses;

■ how to take advantages of opportunities; *and*

■ how to minimise threats.

Corrective action can then be taken.

Increasing focus on the customer has led Sun Life to look at communications as a strategic issue. The company's aim it to make telephone skills the best in the industry.

In 1994 two project groups were set up within Sun Life to establish best practice in telephone communications. An internal research exercise was conducted and a document put together on best practice.

Once standards were set to match best practice, telephone calls were taped to see how employees were performing against the practice standards. The review identified what was happening in practice and why. To reinforce this further, research was commissioned from an outside benchmarking company. Where gaps were identified in practice, training was then provided to relevant employees.

NCR have been involved with benchmarking since 1989 and have formulated a list of key metrics (measurement criteria) for comparison with selected blue-chip companies. At one of their plants, for example, research was carried out and directors and management asked to nominate the most significant metrics. Further research identified potential benchmarking partners who had relevant data and who were willing to share. When NCR reviewed their experiences they discovered that the concentration on blue-chip companies was justified because they were the ones most familiar with benchmarking and tended to operate best practices. Benchmarking activities at NCR have focused on office equipment manufacturers and industries associated with electronics to enable common ground for discussion and exchange of data.

NCR see the benefits in this programme coming from the shared knowledge and likely 'best in class' performance comparisons. Reviewing achievements of benchmarking studies has helped them to target areas for future improvement programmes.[1]

Reviewing the results of learning

In addition to measuring and monitoring the effectiveness of benchmarking programmes in terms of overall improvements in performance within the organisation, the project team should also seek to identify what learning has taken place as a result of the process. A review of the learning that has been achieved in one organisation, for example, identified that benefits to the team and organisation of the study had been:

■ knowledge of what performance is possible;

■ identification and understanding of proven ways of achieving this;

■ thorough understanding of own process;

■ personal development of team members;

■ motivation for change within an organisation; *and*

■ development of network for possible future contracts.

The review of the benefits of benchmarking will help promote the techniques throughout the organisation and give employees the confidence to extend benchmarking to other areas.

At Motorola, for example, the success of benchmarking projects has encouraged further teams to undertake benchmarking initiatives. Benchmarking is concentrated

151

on manufacturing technology. Within this, benchmarking studies have addressed such areas as:

- Automated assembly performance - benchmarked weekly against its Japanese Motorola counterpart, which in turn benchmark against the Japanese sub-contractor.

- Warehouse performance - in particular cycle time, quality, productivity and space used against other Motorola installations.

- Purchasing performance - both against Motorola companies and friendly companies outside the group.

- Salary and benefits packages - through a Motorola initiated exchange of data with other Scottish manufacturing companies.[2]

KEEPING UP TO DATE

In order to keep benchmarking information up to date a number of benchmarking networks have been established. Here groups of individuals representing their companies meet on a regular basis to share information, successes and failures.

If you do form a network where possible keep the numbers of participants in such networking groups small. Remember, however, that attendance rates at meetings can be as low as 50 per cent!

Strict confidentiality should be a prerequisite of membership so that participants are able to share their experiences openly - both good and bad.

Benchmarking networks are only as beneficial as the input from their membership. Geoff Rogers of Standard Chartered explains 'Sitting in the head office of a global business, it is an extremely important means to keep in touch with people who are facing similar cross border problems ... but it only works because there is total trust between members of the group and we have the same mind-set in what we are trying to achieve from bench-marking.'[3]

Strategic overview

As best practices are ever changing, it is helpful to keep abreast of developments in the external market. To this end some organisations appoint someone in a strategic position who can take an overview of external developments and relate these back to the organisation. This type of benchmarking on a strategic level can help the business address longer term issues of competitive advantage.

Extending benchmarking

Once a benchmarking study has been completed and a review has taken place a project team can identify further areas throughout the business where benchmarking will be of benefit. In addition to identifying areas of further studies, it is also helpful to discuss what training needs will be required in order to undertake further bench-marking studies. It is unlikely, for example, that the same project team will have the appropriate experience to benchmark in a different area of the business.

Benchmarking works best when it is done in a context of experimental and action-centred learning and where experiences can be shared. The team needs to consider how to use its learning to extend benchmarking to other areas of the business and how to find champions for the cause.

Benchmarking champions

As we have seen earlier, senior management commitment is particularly important to the process and the project team will do well to review the extent of this commitment. However, benchmarking works best where there are champions throughout all levels of the business.

Hawker Fuse Gear is part of the Hawker Siddley Group. Benchmarking takes place at its 300-employee Burton-on-the-Wold site, where it makes high and low voltage fuse lines. Its benchmarking initiative was originally inspired by Rank Xerox's presentation to a British Quality Association management group. Continued networking with other British Quality Association members has helped to define the research process.

Acquisition of fuse and fuse-fitting companies in both the UK and US has enabled benchmarking within the group not only of products but also of systems. The results have been ready interchange of information, particularly by the respective quality managers. One person who has championed the search for best practices has been the Burton-on-the-Wold Site Quality Manager.

An active member of the best practice benchmarking programme, he can often be seen in places like the local Argos Catalogue Store checking order picks per hour or even at a local brickyard checking contract preview procedures. As he explains, 'It is the duty of every manager in industry to say – Is this the best I can do? If he sees something better he should emulate it, then improve it.'[4]

SUMMARY

- Benchmarking project teams should take care to review the progress of the programme in terms of organisational performance and the learning that has been gained from the process.

- Joining a benchmarking network or appointing someone to take a strategic overview is helpful in keeping abreast of best practice initiatives.

■ Once a successful benchmarking study has been completed, organisations should look for further measures to benchmark and who will champion the cause throughout the business.

CHECKLIST

Use this checklist to help you plan how to put the key points from the chapter to use within your organisation.

1. Hold a review of your benchmarking study to date. Use the question checklist on pages 148-9 to review results.

2. Prepare a SWOT analysis of the project.

3. Identify what learning has taken place as a result of the benchmarking project and how this can be extended to other areas.

4. Join a benchmarking networking group.

5. Appoint someone in a strategic position within the organisation to take an overview of the process.

6. Identify champions who can promote benchmarking throughout the organisation.

REFERENCES

1. DTI Publications, *Managing into the '90s: Best Practice Benchmarking*.
2. DTI Publications, *Managing into the '90s: Best Practice Benchmarking*.
3. Syrett, M (Winter 1993-4) 'The Best of Everything', *Human Resources*, Issue No. 12, page 86.
4. DTI Publications, *Managing in the '90s: Best Practice Benchmarking*.

10

Managing benchmarking in your organisation

Ever since Rank Xerox became trail-blazers of benchmarking in the late 1970s and 1980s, management consultants have predicted that benchmarking will revolutionise organisational performance.

Soon after Xerox's benchmarking efforts were chronicled by Richard Camp, interest in the topic was high enough for the International Benchmarking Clearing House to be formed. Membership currently stands at around 300 organisations.

Benchmarking became an integral part of the US Malcolm Baldridge Quality Awards. The topic took off to such an extent that in the United States television commercials referred to their products as 'best in class'!

In Europe and South America many organisations are now following suit and using benchmarking as a strategic tool.

However, research in the United States has found that although the concept is well known to managers, few companies are engaging in systematic benchmarking studies.

LESSONS FROM LEADING EDGE BENCHMARKING COMPANIES

What makes the management of benchmarking studies so difficult? There are a number of key success criteria which have been identified by benchmarking practitioners.

1. Link benchmarking to the organisation's mission

Organisations who use benchmarking to best effect do so because it is seen as a tool to assist them to achieve their corporate mission. Where benchmarking studies are undertaken as a one-off unsystematic exercise with little relevance to the organisation's objectives, there can be few long-lasting effects.

2. Set measurable objectives

Successful benchmarking organisations identify clearly what they wish to achieve from the study, both in terms of organisational learning and development as well as individual gains.

3. Gain senior management commitment

Senior managers need to believe in the process and its benefits and take an active part in the programme. Unless there is support from the highest level of the organisation, recommendations from the benchmarking study will be hard to achieve.

4. Create a powerful team

The team which conducts benchmarking studies needs to have sufficient influence throughout the organisation to be able to effect change. Its members need training and support to drive the process through.

5. Focus on the right issues

Once the project team has been formed, it needs to understand the process fully and focus on the right

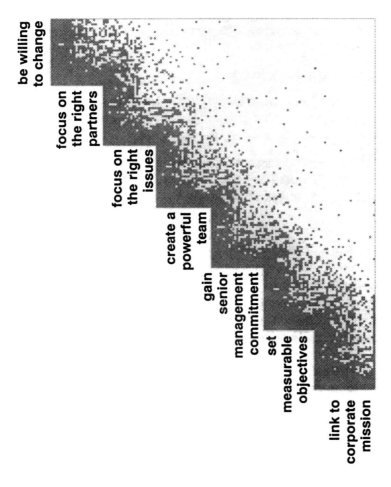

Figure 10.1 *7 steps to success in the benchmarking process*

be willing
to change

focus on
the right
partners

focus on
the right
issues

create a
powerful
team

gain
senior
management
commitment

set
measurable
objectives

link to
corporate
mission

issues. This will ensure the team asks the right questions of benchmarking partners.

6. Focus on the right partners

Benchmarking study results will only be as good as the quality of the benchmarking partners. Careful research and selection of partners is key to benchmarking success.

7. Be willing to change

Once the benchmarking study has been completed, organisations must be prepared to take on board the recommendations from the findings.

Change is not easy and requires careful management. The benchmarking study will only prove as useful as the improvements that result from it.

Continuous improvement

The success stories for benchmarking focus on the need to benchmark on a continuous basis.

As John Towers, Managing Director of The Rover Group, states, 'Part of the business of corporate learning is to learn from the best anywhere. There is no shame in that ... the only shame in this life is ignorance.'

Benchmarking should be a normal part of organisational life. It has to be a continuous activity as what is best practice today may not be so tomorrow.

BENCHMARKING IN ACTION: CASE STUDIES

Two organisations have successfully used benchmarking strategically and to improve internal processes.

Royal Mail

Royal Mail has an annual turnover of £4 billion and almost 180,000 staff. Daily, it handles over 63 million items of mail to its customers nationwide. Over the last few years customers have seen increased quality of service with over 93 per cent of first class letters now delivered next day. Royal Mail has had 17 consecutive years of subsidy-free profit.

In September 1988, Royal Mail began its total quality programme called 'Customer First'. Since then it has completed a massive training programme for all its management, administration and front-line staff in the principles and techniques of total quality and is progressively involving all staff in continuous improvement.

Background

Royal Mail's aim is consistently to satisfy agreed customer requirements. The business recognises that requirements change due to:

■ the passage of time;

■ the actions and performance of competitors; *and*

■ wider changes in the marketplace.

Royal Mail required a system to examine how 'market leaders' achieved outstanding performance.

Five years into the quality initiative, Royal Mail has developed and deployed many of the approaches and techniques encompassed by TQM. In the early stage of its TQ initiative Royal Mail learned from the Rank Xerox experience and identified benchmarking as a powerful way to enhance business performance.

Royal Mail is following a TQM path to excellence. The process encompasses Self Assessment, Customer Quality Measures and Process Understanding which leads to benchmarking of 'world class' organisations.

In a large company such as Royal Mail several forms of benchmarking have been undertaken. Initially many of Royal Mail's senior managers were involved in looking at other organisations (mainly in the US) which were known to excel in total quality. The companies were identified through their involvement in the Malcolm Baldridge Quality Award or their achievements in implementing total quality.

Royal Mail refers to this method of learning from other companies on their policies and approach as Strategic Benchmarking. It is differentiated from Best Practice Benchmarking which is concerned with processes.

The identified need to become actively involved in benchmarking encouraged Royal Mail to develop its own benchmarking process which built on its own research and the experience of Xerox. This process has been the central core of all its benchmarking activity.

Royal Mail puts emphasis on sharing and learning from the good ideas and practices within the company, and improvement teams are supported and encouraged to benchmark across the business. A good example of this is the annual teamwork events. These events allow improvement teams, from across Royal Mail, to come together and exhibit and share their projects with colleagues. Royal Mail refers to this as Internal Best Practice Benchmarking and sees it as a very powerful and useful tool. However, barriers to this activity exist, such as the 'not invented here syndrome'.

Critical Success Factors

Before starting its 'Customer First' initiative, Royal Mail carried out a comprehensive Current State review of all factors important to its business; namely, its markets, customers, products, processes, culture, people and leadership.

Leadership was prioritised as one fundamental key to the successful implementation of TQM and was therefore defined as a Critical Success Factor for the business.

Step 1: Choose process to be benchmarked

The implementation of total quality in Royal Mail reached a point where its understanding of the basics was great enough that it could learn from the policies and processes of companies who were further down the TQ road. Royal Mail hoped its approach to leadership would be more effective and efficient by introducing new ideas and avoiding blind alleys through understanding the mistakes of others.

Step 2: Who to benchmark against?

To determine who to benchmark against Royal Mail turned to those companies which clearly demonstrated achievements in total quality and which had been recognised through the Malcolm Baldridge awards. It identified Motorola, Westinghouse, IBM and Milliken as companies to benchmark against. The gap between Royal Mail and selected companies was measured by its Current State Review and the standards required to gain the Baldridge award.

Step 3: Who should participate in the activity?

The criteria established for participation in the study tour activity were:

- completion of basic training in total quality;

- ability to implement directly, where appropriate, many of the lessons learned and to influence others; *and*

- provide a balance of directors, general managers and field managers covering most key areas of Royal Mail.

The members of these early groups have gone on to be very influential within Royal Mail not only in benchmarking but in all other areas of total quality.

Step 4: What preparation was completed ahead of the tour?

Each of the selected companies was contacted to gain their agreement to the visits and to what would be involved, as follows:

■ describe their overall approach and the key area of leadership;

■ provide background information on the company (this was reciprocated by Royal Mail);

■ sub group of Royal Mail managers identified and prepared for visit;

■ used Baldridge category on leadership as a checklist; *and*

■ planned to work together after the visit to identify potential improvements.

Step 5: What was learnt from the companies?

The 'Code of Conduct' followed by companies which were benchmarking prevents release of information other than of a general nature without prior consent. Royal Mail found most companies were happy to release information, much of which is not commercially sensitive.

The purpose of the benchmarking study was to identify characteristics of effective leadership. Some examples of aspects of leadership observed are as follows:

■ managers as facilitators of self managing teams;

■ clear leadership of total quality by chief executive;

■ strong focus on recognition at all levels;

■ lots of Managing by Wandering Around (MBWA);

■ managers selected for their respect for the abilities of people; *and*

- communication skills, low desire for total control, and staying power.

Step 6: Overall debriefing and action plan development

On return from the tour, team members were required to document key learning points, recommend actions and share these with colleagues. Following the initial synthesis and development of preliminary recommendations the team met to review its actions which led to specific recommendations for action to the Chief Executive's Committee.

Step 7: Review and ongoing relationship

The sessions with these leading-edge companies strengthened Royal Mail's view that the initial steps taken were sound. This represented the start of an ongoing relationship with these companies and while most of the learning was achieved by Royal Mail there were several areas where Royal Mail's experience was of interest to the host companies. The progress of the recommendations is also regularly reviewed.

Best practice benchmarking

Following Royal Mail's Strategic Benchmarking of Leadership in the early 1990s and the initial development of Management Behaviour and Feedback Systems and a Management Charter, the business identified a need to measure effective leadership using Best Practice Benchmarking (or Operational Process Benchmarking).

Step 0: Build team and plan

The team consisted mostly of Quality Managers because the process to be benchmarked was mainly operated by them. The benchmarking team was already in existence and working on a Quality Improvement Project on leadership supported at a senior level within Royal Mail.

Step 1: Select process

The existing process for measurement and feedback of leadership in Royal Mail was called the 'Management Behaviour Feedback System' (MBFS) and had been used since 1988 as a continuation of the initial TQ training. The format was 'upward appraisal' from team members to their manager, but the process had decayed for a number of reasons and was no longer operating effectively.

A 'Leadership Charter' was being developed separately and the need for a suitable measurement process for the charter was seen as a Critical Success Factor.

Step 2: Describe process

The current process was 'mapped' and areas of performance weakness identified. Royal Mail found that process mapping is a time-consuming step in the benchmarking process, but its importance cannot be overstated. It can potentially contribute to more improvement to the organisation and its output than any other step.

Some areas of performance weakness in the current process are highlighted below:

- simpler marking frame;
- simpler questions;
- less support time from Quality Managers;
- links to annual performance appraisal; *and*
- able to use six-monthly.

Step 3: Identification of target organisations

Using personal team member contacts, business articles, quality organisation networking and other 'data sources' a number of organisations were identified as potential benchmarks.

- WH Smith

- Holiday Inns

- Tom Peters Group

- Avis

- Babcocks

From these data sources an analysis of the perceived gap in performance was developed. This enabled the team to prepare specific objectives for each of the potential benchmark organisations and to prioritise the planned benchmarking activities.

Step 4: Preparation

Initial contact with each company was via telephone. An agreement in principle with WH Smith and Avis allowed the team to move into more detailed preparation.

This typically involved the following sub process steps:

- agreed terms of reference with target organisation;

- identified appropriate materials for sharing eg, process maps;

- developed questions and checklists for site visits; *and*

- team for visit agreed by both companies.

Step 5: Interaction with benchmark organisation

In this case, contact with the organisations followed three stages. A 'start-up meeting', the actual 'site visit' and a follow up or 'close down' meeting.

Some highlights from the interaction with WH Smith and Avis were:

Avis

- Team leader led the process with support from others.

- Their process included a 'peer group' workshop step.

- Feedback was confidential to team leader.

WH Smith

- Questions developed from what employees felt was important.

- Team members able to select six most important behaviours.

- Only 32 questions in the questionnaire.

The process features, including these highlights, were developed in the new Royal Mail process.

Step 6: Evaluation

The Quality Improvement Project team evaluated the learning points from the interactions with the benchmark companies. This included analysis of results of the process, identification of the actual (rather than perceived) gap in performance/process and the production of reports to assist the next stage of integration.

Step 7: Integration

Royal Mail has several 'change processes' which are used to assist with the integration of benchmark results in the organisation. The most common type and the one used in this case was their Quality Improvement Process, which is similar to the Deming wheel (see page 40). This process positions benchmarking activity in two ways; firstly as a source of 'improvement opportunity', and secondly as a method of 'integrating' step changes into work processes at the 'planning' stage of the improvement cycle.

In the case of the 'Effective Leadership Feedback' process the findings were internally communicated both at the outset and when subsequent training on the new process occurred.

Step 8: Review

A key feature of Royal Mail's basic improvement cycle is the principle of 'continuous improvement' and as such it is envisaged that the new process (launched in 1993) will be re-prioritised as a potential improvement opportunity. The links with their benchmarking partners will also be developed through time for mutual benefit.

Conclusion

This case study has illustrated how a 'structured approach' to benchmarking was deployed by Royal Mail. It may be argued that the need for this approach is fundamental if organisations wish to avoid the potential pitfalls of unplanned, unfocused and haphazard bench-marking activities, which lead to wasted time and effort.

This is not to say that more informal contact between organisations is of no value, but positions true bench-marking as a more formal and disciplined approach.

In conclusion, Royal Mail has identified a number of key indicators for successful benchmarking:

- Comprehensive understanding of how one's own work is conducted.

- Willingness to change based on benchmarking findings.

- Realisation that competition is constantly changing.

- Willingness to share information.

- A focus on customer service best practices and latterly performance measures.

- Continuous benchmarking effort.[1]

---

[1] Reproduced by kind permission of Walter Crosbie, Royal Mail Scotland and Northern Ireland.

British Airways

British Airways is an example of an organisation which has successfully used benchmarking in three ways; to learn from the competition, to improve internal processes and to identify best practice.

The starting point for benchmarking is that the organisation *must* change, and change radically. Twelve years ago, British Airways was not listening sufficiently to customers. They had become complacent. The crisis was that they had lost around half a billion pounds. The need was to focus on the customer.

Competitive benchmarking

In l983, in order to develop a 'Putting the Customer First' campaign, British Airways looked around at a number of other companies which had brought themselves closer to their customers. This was the start for the relaunch of British Airways. It was at this stage that British Airways began benchmarking. They were seeking excellence in training staff to be more responsive to customers. They identified organisations which had done this and followed their example to train staff to become more customer focused. Sources of information for identifying excellence were less extensive then than now but reputation was relevant. Management magazines, executive surveys, consultancy contacts, self-help groups, all were and are relevant in surveying the world's enterprises for comparators.

British Airways found that before setting out on to benchmark you must be clear as to the aim. Survey data and gut feeling told British Airways their focus should be on customers. Each month British Airways analyse survey data and customers' complaints in great detail. Currently, for example, their customers tell British Airways they need to improve how they handle flight disruption situations. This is just one source of information for assessing priorities.

Other data must be taken into account. British Airways survey their staff to identify their major concerns. Similarly they must act on the interests of the third category of stakeholders, the owners and finance providers. Commitment to the need for improvement based on these priorities indicates the radical steps required.

In setting up a benchmarking study, British Airways train the team in analysing the relevant activities and charting these in detail. Without full understanding of your own company's processes, external comparison is of limited value. For 'airport arrivals', for example, the benchmarking team included monitoring the service they deliver, adding value to the service, delivering bags, confirming the travel at reservations. The team used formal charting techniques to ensure that results were objective and visible. Their comparison covered detailed visits and discussions with seven other organisations. Significant improvements have been made as a result, spurred on by the experience of the participants.

British Airways used Deming's four stages – Plan, Do, Check, Act – to highlight the elements of this approach. They have found that benchmarking needs the commitment to radical change and the understanding of their own processes in order to undertake beneficial benchmarking which will have lasting impact.

Functional benchmarking

The second element of British Airways' approach to benchmarking encompasses functional benchmarking to improve internal processes. Processes such as management communications and feedback occur in all organisations. In looking at how the management style affected morale and stimulated better performance, British Airways sought examples from service organisations worldwide, having first noted the stage of development they had reached.

Functional benchmarking requires understanding of the organisation's processes. Behind British Airways' activities, there are eleven major processes. Hosting the customer is one. All customer service activities comprise parts of the business processes that run through British Airways' activity. British Airways have used these process maps to examine what problems lie behind the scenes and how they link to other aspects of their business. They then have a more detailed view of the functional elements which comprise it. Communicating the reason for change is one of the crucial steps. British Airways have found that at least twice the time of the project itself should be spent in the creating of the environment in which it's going to occur.

British Airways' cabin crew are expected to behave in a very friendly way, to look after the customers and respond to their needs. Research in the past found that although customers respond well to the way the cabin crew are treating them, on occasions they find aspects of their service inconsistent. British Airways have undertaken various analyses to try and understand how these symptoms make themselves felt and what the reactions of the crew are. They have spent time trying to create a different structure designed to integrate the communication process.

British Airways have studied other organisations which have done particularly well in motivating their employees. They have designed and trialled a different management arrangement for the crew in the 767 fleet. What they were doing was setting up a different management ethos, based on trust, and one in which they would get the benefit of the different structure, particularly for cabin crew whose 'life style' would be improved by a more humanised rostering system.

British Airways recognised that the communication 'gap' between management and the absent workforce needs to be closed. Management style in this fleet was revolutionised with staff using the fleet office regularly. Procedures were changed as well as changes in personnel. Since the fleet has been in operation, substantial benefits have been achieved from it. Both customer satisfaction and staff morale have improved as employees' working conditions and motivation were addressed.

What did the members of the crew themselves think? It was no good just describing what the organisation was trying to do in setting up this fleet. They had to work to communicate fully the reasons for it, the comparators used and how it would help the crew themselves. They had to convince them of the gap in best practice and the need to overcome some of the obstacles. Best practice of the different companies are demonstrated by the levels of customer satisfaction they achieve. British Airways were interested to show how the changes in management practices would benefit individual crew; the 'what's in it for me' issue.

The success of this initiative has helped in the re-design of the future strategy for all cabin crew. A new structure based on these results is being progressively introduced this year.

Generic best practice benchmarking

A project team was set up to introduce a focused engineering unit geared to the production of high value, reliable and consistent maintenance services.

To learn from the best, the project team surveyed five generic benchmarks. Specific contacts were made through in-depth studies associated with British Airways' in-house MBA programme.

The objective of the team was to develop a small-scale organisation to realise products more quickly and encourage staff groups to take greater responsibility. These generic benchmarks were drawn from a wide range of industries. Some have been formalised into a longer term relationship of data exchange and joint visits.

Having chosen a location away from British Airways' main activities, the new engineering subsidiary was set up to apply the lessons of the TQM programme developed during the previous five years in the Engineering Department. Specific benchmarks were digested and an organisational structure devised which modelled the best elements from the generic 'best in class' reference points. The aim of the new unit was world-class excellence.

The operation began with a single production line and 350 employees. By 1994 there were two production lines and a very satisfactory 'learning curve' progress with productivity. The quality of output is high with 'ownership' a crucial lever in stimulating community spirit and output quality. Generic benchmarking with 'best in class' partners has helped achieve these results.[2]

SUMMARY

■ This chapter outlines seven steps to the successful management of the benchmarking process.

■ It concludes with case studies of two organisations which have successfully put benchmarking to great effect in their companies.

CHECKLIST

Use this checklist to help you plan how to put the key points from the chapter to use within your organisation.

1. Contact organisations which are currently using benchmarking as a catalyst for change.

2. Identify the learning that has taken place in these organisations and how this can be applied to your business.

---

[2]Reproduced by kind permission of Roger Davies, British Airways.

Sources of further information

Department of Trade and Industry

The DTI's Enterprise Initiative offers businesses a co-ordinated programme of information, advice and assisted consultancies on key areas of best management practice. The DTI initiative, Inside UK Enterprise, provides an opportunity to visit leading companies employing best practice, in a wide range of product areas. All visits are designed to give a better understanding of the various processes involved and to provide a forum in which to discuss with senior management the implications of the advanced technology and the strategic issues which help to create business success.

Department of Trade and Industry
Kingsgate House, Bay 511
66–74 Victoria Street
London SW1E 6SW
Tel: (0171) 215 8142

DTI Quality Assurance (QA) Register

The DTI QA Register lists around 12,000 companies in the UK and abroad whose quality systems have been assessed to ISO 9000 (or an equivalent standard) by a UK-certification body. The Register can be obtained from HMSO retail outlets.

Employment Department

The Training and Enterprise Councils (TECs) of the Employment Department are Britain's national authority for vocational education and training and the Employment Department annually rewards excellence in training with the National Training Awards. Contact your nearest Training and Enterprise Council office for information.

British Standards Institution (BSI)

BSI is responsible for preparing British Standards which are used in all industries and technologies. It also represents British interests at international standards discussions to ensure that European and worldwide standards will be acceptable to British industry.

Enquiry Section
BSI
Linford Wood
Milton Keynes MK14 6LE
Tel: (01908) 221166

The British Quality Association (BQA)

The BQA exists to promote a better understanding of quality throughout industry and commerce. Membership is open to all industrial, commercial and other corporate organisations.

215 Vauxhall Bridge Road
London SW1V 1EN
Tel: (0171) 963 8000

The European Foundation for Quality Management

The Foundation for Quality Management promotes total quality throughout the European Community.

190 Avenue les Pleiades
1200 Brussels
Belgium
Tel: 0032 277 91 717

Benchmarking Clearing Houses

The International Benchmarking Clearing House run by IFS International in the UK offers a means of forming local and international partnerships. It hosts common interest groups, provides a clearing house database and network meetings and publications.

International Benchmarking Clearing House
IFS International Ltd
Wolseley Business Park
Kempston
Bedford MK42 7PW
Tel: (01234) 853605

Benchmarking Centre Ltd.

The centre acts as a clearing house and provides useful information on the benchmarking process.

c/o Dexion Ltd.
Marylands Avenue
Hemel Hempstead
Herts HP2 7EW
Tel: (01442) 250040

Organisations with an interest in benchmarking

The following organisations can provide further information on various aspects of benchmarking.

Financial benchmarks

ICC Information Group
Financial Surveys
Field House
72 Oldfield Road
Hampton
Middlesex TW12 2HQ
Tel: (0181) 783 0988

Strategic Planning Institute
PIMS Associates
7th Floor
Moor House
199 London Wall
London EC27 5ET
Tel: (0171) 628 1155

Personnel, compensations etc.

Reward Regional Surveys
Reward Group
Reward House
Diamond Way
Stone Business Park
Stone
Buckinghamshire ST15 OSD
Tel: (01785) 813566

Incomes Data Services

193 St John Street
London EC1V 4LS
Tel: (0171) 250 3434

Towers Perrin
Castlewood House
77–91 New Oxford Street
London WC1A 1PX
Tel: (0171) 379 4411

Hay Management Consultants
52 Grosvenor Gardens
London SW1W 0AU
Tel: (0171) 730 0833

Study tours relevant to benchmarking

Dave Hutchins Associates
13/14 Hermitage Parade
High Street
Ascot SL5 7HE
Tel: (01344) 28712

PA Consulting Group
123 Buckingham Palace Road
London SW1W 9SR
Tel: (0171) 730 9000

IFS Conferences
Wolsley Business Park
Wolsley Road
Kempton
Bedford MK42 7PW
Tel: (01234) 853605

Bibliography

Bendell, T, Kelly, J and Merry, T (1993) Quality Measuring and Monitoring, Century Business, London

Bendell, T, Boulter, L and Kelly, J (1993) Benchmarking for Competitive Advantage, Pitman in association with the Financial Times, London

Bogan, C E and English, M J (1994) Benchmarking for Best Practices: Winning Through Innovative Adaption, McGraw Hill, Maidenhead

Boxwell, R J (1994) Benchmarking for Competitive Advantages, McGraw Hill, Maidenhead

Camp, R C (1989) Benchmarking: The Search for Industry Best Practices that Lead to Superior Performances, American Society for Quality Control (ASQC) Quality Press, New York

Chang, R and Keyy, K (1994) 'Improving through benchmarking', Richard Chang Associates Inc, USA

Coding, S (1992) 'Best practice benchmarking: the management guide to successful implementation', Industrial Newsletters Ltd, Bedford

Coopers & Lybrand (1994) Survey of benchmarking in the UK: Executive Summary, Confederation of British Industry, London

The Economist (11 May 1991) 'First find your bench'

Fitz-Enz, J (1993) Benchmarking Staff Performance: How Staff Departments can Enhance their value to the Customer, Jossey Bass, New York

Fuld, L M (1988) Monitoring the Competition, John Wiley & Sons, London

Karlof, B and Ostblom, S (1993) Benchmarking: A Signpost to Excellence in Quality and Productivity, John Wiley & Sons, London

McNair, C J and Leibfried, K H J (1992) Benchmarking: A Tool for Continuous Improvement' Harper Business, London

Miller, J, Meyer, DE and Nakane, J (1992) Benchmarking Global Manufacturing, Homewood, Illinois

Russell, J P (1993) Quality Management Benchmark Assessment, IFS Publications, Dunstable

Walleck, A et al (1991) 'Benchmarking world-class performance', The McKinsey Quarterly, No 1, USA

Watson, G H (1993) Strategic Benchmarking: How to Rate your Company's Performance against the World's Best', John Wiley & Sons, London

Zairi, Dr M (1992) Competitive Benchmarking: An Executive Guide, Technical Communications (Publishing) Ltd, London

Zairi, Dr M and Leonard, P (1994) Practical Benchmarking: A Complete Guide, Chapman & Hall, Cambridge

Magazines

The Benchmark, published by IFS International. Tel: 01234-853605

Videos

Benchmarking to Win, Financial Times Business Tool Kit Video, Training Direct. Tel: 01279-623927

Index

Printed in the United Kingdom
by Lightning Source UK Ltd.
124400UK00002B/184-192/A